D1304423

Chemically speaking,
chocolate really is
the world's perfect food.

—

Michael Levine, nutrition researcher,
as quoted in *The Emperors of Chocolate:
Inside the Secret World of Hershey and Mars*

WHEN CHOCOLATE Isn't ENOUGH

ISBN 978-1-61795-479-5

Published by Worthy Inspired, an imprint of Worthy Publishing Group, a division of Worthy Media, Inc.
134 Franklin Road, Suite 200, Brentwood, Tennessee 37027.

Scripture references marked KJV are from the Holy Bible, King James Version

Scripture references marked NKJV are from the Holy Bible, New King James Version. Copyright © 1982 by Thomas Nelson, Inc. Used by permission.

Scripture references marked NCV are from the New Century Version®. Copyright © 1987, 1988, 1991 by Word Publishing, a division of Thomas Nelson, Inc. All rights reserved. Used by permission.

Scripture references marked HCSB are from the Holman Christian Standard Bible™ Copyright © 1999, 2000, 2001 by Holman Bible Publishers. Used by permission.

Scripture references marked NIV are from the Holy Bible, New International Version®, NIV® Copyright © 1973, 1978, 1984, 2011 by Biblica, Inc.® Used by permission. All rights reserved worldwide.

Scripture references marked NRSV are from the New Revised Standard Version Bible, Copyright © 1989 the Division of Christian Education of the National Council of the Churches of Christ in the United States of America. Used by permission. All rights reserved.

Scripture references marked ESV are from the Holy Bible, English Standard Version, Copyright © 2001 by Crossway Bibles, a division of Good News Publishers.

Scripture references marked NASB are from the New American Standard Bible®, Copyright © 1960, 1962, 1963, 1968, 1971, 1972, 1973, 1975, 1977, 1995 by The Lockman Foundation. Used by permission.

Scripture references marked TLB are from the Holy Bible, The Living Bible, Copyright © 1971 owned by assignment by Illinois Regional Bank N.A. (as trustee). Used by permission of Tyndale House Publishers, Inc., Wheaton, Illinois 60189. All rights reserved.

Scripture references marked NLT are from the Holy Bible. New Living Translation. Copyright © 1996 Tyndale Charitable Trust. Used by permission of Tyndale House Publishers.

Scripture references marked MSG are from the Message. Copyright © 1993, 1994, 1995, 1996, 2000, 2001, 2002. Used by permission of NavPress Publishing Group.

Cover Design by Kim Russell / Wahoo Designs
Page Layout by Bart Dawson

Printed in the United States of America

1 2 3 4 5—LBM—19 18 17 16 15

WHEN CHOCOLATE Isn't ENOUGH

AN INSPIRATIONAL
SURVIVAL GUIDE FOR MOMS

MICHELLE MEDLOCK ADAMS

WORTHY
Inspired

In memory of my sweet, chocolate-loving mother,
Marion Medlock.

For my two precious daughters, Abby and Allyson.
You inspire me every day, and there's no one else
I'd rather share a "Death by Chocolate" dessert with
than you two . . . love you both so much! —*Mom*

All I really need is love,
but a little chocolate
now and then doesn't hurt!

—

Lucy Van Pelt in "Peanuts" by Charles M. Schulz

CHOCOLATE—
THE FLAVOR OF MY LIFE

I pushed through the crowd of other pony-tailed girls for a glimpse at—the list. It had been four hours since freshman cheerleading tryouts, and now was the moment of truth. Out of 64 girls vying for six spots on the Bedford North Lawrence High School Freshman Cheer Team, had I made it? My eyes scanned each number—*where's 23?* I looked down at the number on my chest, just to make sure it didn't match any of the six numbers on the list, but I already knew the answer. I hadn't made the squad. I'd been cheerleader in fifth, sixth, seventh, and eighth grade, but I'd have to sit on the sidelines my freshman year. I felt like I'd been run over by a huge truck and then backed up over again. I congratulated the girls in the corner who were already celebrating their accomplishment of making the squad, and then I walked out the gym door toward Mom's car. She'd been waiting patiently. It was one of the longest walks of my life.

Before I could utter the words, "I didn't make it," she already knew.

Mom didn't say a word, she just reached over and hugged me. As we drove home, the car was silent except for the short bursts of sobbing coming from my side of the car. Then, she stopped in downtown Bedford.

"What are you doing?" I asked, wiping the mascara from my face.

"I'll be right back," she said, hustling into a nearby store.

When Mom returned, she had a bag from Hoover's Candy Store. She handed it to me and said, "Go ahead. Dig in! Life is too short to be sad."

I smiled as I peered into the little white paper bag to find double-dipped chocolate covered peanuts—my all-time favorite candy in the world!

"Thanks," I said, while biting into my first double-dipped delicacy.

And so the tradition began. Anytime, there was something in life to get over or something in life to celebrate—we did it with chocolate. We didn't overdo it. A truffle here. A turtle there. But, the tradition remained strong throughout my life.

When I decided to try out for cheerleader again my senior year and made the Varsity squad, we drove straight to Hoover's Candy Shop and celebrated with—you guessed it—double-dipped, chocolate covered peanuts. Years later when my husband and I found out we were having a baby girl, Mom dropped off chocolate treats with pink cream filling in honor of the glorious news. When Mom won the City Golf Tournament, we split a chocolate dessert called "Death by Chocolate" at a nearby restaurant. They say what doesn't kill you makes you stronger!

I'd have to agree.

Chocolate became our secret bond, though we didn't need anything to keep us close. My mother and I had always been best friends. Still, sharing chocolate treats somehow linked us together even when miles separated us. When my husband and our daughters and I moved to Texas for my job, leaving Mom and Dad behind in Indiana was very hard. I missed them terribly. After all, they had lived right next door to us for several years, and now, it seemed, we were dozens of states away. One day while unpacking one of the many boxes in our new home in Texas, the doorbell rang. It was UPS, dropping off a package for me.

As I tore open the box, I immediately recognized the small white box with the gold label—it was from Hoover's. The card read, "Thought you might need a little extra energy for all of your unpacking. Love you, Mom." The chocolate turtles tasted so wonderful—better than I had remembered. I savored each one over the next few days.

CHOCOLATE-COVERED MEMORIES

Over the years, Mom and I baked chocolate cookies, split rich chocolate desserts, cheated on our diets with York Peppermint Patties, and enjoyed each other's company every time we were together. Even when Mom received the bad report from the doctor, we dealt with the cancer diagnosis with a few bites of chocolate ice cream. As Mom battled the disease and I sat next to her hospital bed, I wanted to relive every single chocolate-covered memory. I wanted to savor every silly thing we'd ever done and remember every funny thing she'd ever said. Neither one of us had an appetite, and Mom wasn't keeping much down, but when she woke up that afternoon, she looked up at me and whispered, "I could sure go for a chocolate milkshake." I smiled down at her and said, "Done. I'll be right back." The wonderful kitchen staff at the hospital listened as I shared my mom's love for chocolate and agreed to make Mom a hand-dipped chocolate milkshake—even though it wasn't on the menu.

"This is good," she said, sipping her shake. "Take a drink, honey."

"OK," I said, using my own straw.

It was so thick I could hardly get it through the skinny straw but it was certainly worth the work. Wow, was it yummy! As we sipped her chocolate shake, we shared yet another tender time together—one that I wouldn't trade for all the chocolate in the world. Mom went to heaven in May 2006, and I have to believe that she has some divine double-dipped chocolate covered peanuts awaiting my arrival. Until then, I'll continue the chocolate tradition with my own daughters and remember the words Mom spoke to me the day the chocolate tradition began: "Go ahead. Dig in! Life is too short to be sad."

I hope as you read this book, you'll "dig in" and be encouraged on this wonderful journey we call motherhood. Whether you're a new mom or an empty-nester, we're all in this together! And, isn't it a blessing?

To be honest, I wasn't one of those girls who grew up longing to be a mom, naming my future children, and dreaming about playdates and pacifiers. But, I am so thankful that God saw past my false pride and infinite insecurities and allowed me to be a mother because I cannot imagine my life without my girls.

They are my life!

And, while being a mom is an amazing blessing, there are days when I really need to hear from God, sit in my favorite chair, and enjoy a Snickers and a Diet Coke to gain perspective again.

Because it's not easy.

Being a mom is the most exhausting, aggravating, joyous, rewarding job you'll ever have, and it all goes by in a big blur of wonderfulness. That's why I wrote this book—as a reminder that we should enjoy the journey; that we are all in this together; that it's a blessing to be a mama; that we can do what God has called us to do; and that having a piece a chocolate along the way is always a good idea.

As the title of this book indicates, yes, this is a "Survival Guide" for us, but we're moms! We do more than survive—we thrive! We are mothers, hear us roar! And, we can do all things through Christ who strengthens us, amen?

I've prayed over these entries. I've prayed over you. And, I don't believe you're reading this book by mistake. I believe that God will use this book to speak to you, encourage you, and give you more joy (and chocolate) for the journey. ☺

THE BITTERSWEET
BALANCING ACT . . .

LEARNING TO EMBRACE
THE CRAZY LIFE WE CALL
"MOTHERHOOD"

Anyone who knows me knows that cooking is definitely not one of my strengths. I cook a few things well, but it's a short list. I do, however, love to bake—especially if there is chocolate involved. That said, I only have a few "tried and true" dessert recipes that I make over and over again for every family get-together and church function. So, when we decided to include yummy chocolate dessert recipes in this book, I enlisted the help of some of my closest friends and family. And trust me, these folks know how to cook!

MY COUSIN LAURA LOU BEMUS

Laura Lou, like me, is into easy and quick desserts so she offered one of her favorites, "Choco Candy Drops."

"When I taught kindergarten, one of the moms brought these in, and they were wonderful," she said. "Then, when I found out how easy they were to make, I started making them quite often for special school treats."

After learning these treats are easy to make and look like you've spent a lot of time on them, I just knew we had to have them in this book.

CHOCO CANDY DROPS

4 tablespoons butter

½ cup milk

2 cups sugar

¼ cup cocoa

¾ cup peanut butter

2 cups quick cooking oatmeal

Melt butter in a medium size saucepan. Stir in milk, sugar, and cocoa. Bring to a boil stirring constantly. Remove from heat. Add peanut butter; stir to melt. Mix in oatmeal. Drop from a tablespoon onto wax paper-covered cookie sheet. The mixture will seem thin. Yield: 2 to 3 dozen.

Chapter 1

GOD'S GOT TIME . . . DO YOU?

I often wonder why God wouldn't have created mothers with at least ten sets of hands and a couple of extra hours a day. Seriously, though, is there anyone busier than a mom? My girls are only 20 months apart, and when they were little, I'd pray that somehow I'd be able to squeeze in a shower before nightfall. Maybe that's why I laughed so hard when I read this post on Facebook that said: "All of these moms are on Pinterest making their own soap and reindeer-shaped treats, and I'm like, 'I took a shower and kept the kids alive.'" Maybe you can relate. From preparing meals to bath time to playtime to cleaning the house to doing laundry to running errands to having at least one meaningful conversation with your husband . . . life is crazy busy!

But you know what I discovered early on in this amazing journey we call motherhood? Whenever I make time for God, I somehow supernaturally get everything else on my "To Do List" done! Apparently I'm not alone. I recently read an article by inspirational speaker and author Gloria Copeland, who shared that she had experienced that same phenomena when she and her husband, Kenneth, had moved into a new house early in their marriage. She admitted that she felt overwhelmed. She needed to unpack the sea of boxes surrounding her, as well as care for her two small children. However, in the middle of her very full days, she felt compelled to read through the four gospels, four times in a month. She thought, *How am I ever going to have time to do all of this Bible reading and get this house in order?* Still, she made it a priority. At the end of the month, she had not only accomplished her reading goal, but also unpacked the whole house and refinished a few pieces of furniture, as well! She had given God her time, and He had given it right back to her.

Now that doesn't make any sense in the natural, but it's true! If, like me, you tend to get overwhelmed trying to prioritize everything, give it all to God and ask for His divine intervention. Then, make a decision that you'll spend time with your Heavenly Father—no matter what! I find it's better to schedule my time with God, even writing it in my planner, because it's not always at the same time each day.

I've heard many pastors preach that it's best to start each day with God, spending time reading the Bible and praying first thing in the morning, but if that doesn't seem possible with your busy morning schedule, do what works best for you. Have your quiet time with God after you put the kids down for their afternoon nap. Grab a cup of hot chocolate, your Word of God, and enjoy some special time with the Father. Or, go to bed with your favorite devotional and read God's Word before you go to sleep. Once you get in the habit, you'll crave being with God just as much as you crave chocolate. Because it's during those precious moments spent in God's presence that we find joy, peace, love, strength and wisdom to be a better mom, a better wife, a better sister, a better daughter, a better friend—just plain better. Ask God to help you find time. He will because He longs to be with you, too!

KISSES FROM HEAVEN

In everything you do, put God first, and he will direct you and crown your efforts with success.

Proverbs 3:6 (TLB)

HEART TO HEAVEN

Father, help me prioritize my day so that I can accomplish everything I need to do. Help me to long for Your Word. I love You, God, and I'm so thankful that You always have time for me. In the mighty name of Jesus, Amen.

Chapter 2

JUGGLING IT ALL

"You NEVER come to any of my special activities at school!" Abby, my then 10-year-old, screamed. "You're ALWAYS working!"

I felt as though someone had punched me in the stomach.

"That's not true!" I retaliated. "I went to your art show, and I went to your musical. And, I even attended the Halloween party. In fact, I brought pumpkin cookies with orange sprinkles to that party!"

"Yeah, but you didn't make them," Abby shouted. "You BOUGHT them!"

She was right. I didn't have time to bake my mother's amazing chocolate oatmeal cookies so I'd opted for the festive store-bought pumpkin-shaped cookies. I didn't think Abby would care, but apparently she did.

I retreated to my bedroom to lick my wounds. I hadn't intended to miss "Moms and Muffins" at Abby's school that morning; nevertheless, I had. Abby didn't understand that my editor had put an unreasonable deadline on me that same day. She didn't care that I was working on a very important article at the exact time when all of the other moms were visiting and enjoying muffins. All she knew is that I had let her down. And, I'm sure that wasn't the only time I let her down during her childhood, or even now as an adult child. (She may be 22, but she'll always be my baby girl.)

Being a mom is a tough gig, whether you work outside the home or not, so give yourself a break! You're doing the best you can, and that makes you amazing! You know, as a working mother, I wasn't always able to keep all of the balls in the air, though I tried really hard. And, whenever I dropped a ball, I felt just awful about it. When I disappoint my girls now, I still feel guilty about whatever it is I did or didn't do. How about you? None of us like to let down the people that we love the most.

Motherhood is a 24-7 job, and the demands are never-ending. Of course, the rewards are pretty good, too. But on the days when you do drop a ball, it's hard to see anything except your failure. I know; I speak from experience. I couldn't get that Moms and Muffins morning back. I hated that I'd missed it, but beating myself up over it wasn't going to do any good, either. After a while, I skulked into Abby's bedroom, ignoring the "Stay Out" sign posted on her door, and I apologized for missing the muffin extravaganza. She forgave me, and then I asked God to help me forgive myself so that I could move forward.

If you're feeling like you're a disappointment in the mom department, you probably need to forgive yourself, too. Those Moms and Muffins mornings are a thing of the past for me, but I still find myself feeling awful when I don't have time to edit a college paper for Abby, or when I forget to send Ally the design book I promised to send her. The truth is: we're human, and sometimes we're going to mess up, so don't place unrealistic expectations on yourself, and don't try to do everything on your own. Ask God to help you achieve everything you need to accomplish. From carpools to deadlines to dance recitals to Moms and Muffins—He can keep you sane and smiling through it all. Remember, you can do all things through Christ who gives you strength. No matter how the muffin crumbles, you've got that promise working for you.

KISSES FROM HEAVEN

For I can do everything with the help of Christ who gives me the strength I need.

Philippians 4:13 (NLT)

HEART TO HEAVEN

Lord, thank You for my children. Thank You for my job. And, thank You for helping me to fulfill each role with excellence. I need Your help juggling it all, and I am asking for that help now. I love You, Lord. Amen.

Chapter 3

DATE NIGHT—YES!

Remember date nights?

I actually married my high school sweetheart, Jeff, so I barely remember life without him. But, there were several years when our daughters were toddlers that we certainly didn't feel like sweethearts. We were more like two people who lived in the same house and eventually collapsed in bed next to each other—sometimes with two daughters and a dog between us.

Sound familiar?

Thankfully, I was part of a Bible study for young marrieds and new moms during that season of my life, and I learned something vital every week. One such lesson was this—never stop dating your husband. Make time for him, apart from the children, and keep that romance alive. I remember sitting in that Bible study and wondering how I could possibly find time to date my husband when we barely had time to do anything apart from the absolutely necessary household tasks and child-rearing duties. Our lives had become so busy with work and raising our little girls that we'd lost sight of everything else. We were sort of just going through the motions of life, mumbling "I love you" before drifting off to sleep at night. I wanted to date my husband again. I talked to my wonderful mama about our situation, and she happily volunteered to babysit for us once a week so that Jeff and I could have a date. Sometimes our date night consisted of going to the movies, holding hands, and sharing a large box of Junior Mints. Other times, it was simply cuddling on the couch and catching up on our DVR'd shows. Other times, we spent our date night at a local bookstore, drinking coffee (I don't like coffee, so I was drinking hot chocolate, of course), reading magazines, and being adults in love. No matter what we did, we looked so forward to that time together each week. I truly believe that because we did make an effort to keep the romance alive as we parented our children, that when our girls both left for college recently, and we were back to just the two of us, we transitioned much more easily than many couples do.

I remember right after the girls left and it was just the two of us at breakfast, I looked across the table at him and said, "Now what?" halfway joking, but halfway nervous about the next chapter. Without missing a beat, Jeff shot me a mischievous grin and said, "Now I get you all to myself again."

We've been dating each other like teenagers ever since, but it all started because we decided to make time for one another early on.

I encourage you to do the same. Even if it just means putting your children to bed early one night a week and reserving that time for just you and your spouse to reconnect. Make the investment in your marriage. The payoff is huge! You don't have to spend lots of money on your date nights. If money is tight, borrow a free movie from your local library; pop some microwave popcorn; and cuddle on the couch. Or, if you have a willing grandparent or aunt who wants to babysit for free, pack a picnic and a blanket, and download your favorite music on your iPhone, and enjoy the beauty of the great outdoors. Dinner and dancing under the stars could be just that break from the mundane that you both need to rekindle the romance.

Here's the thing. If you and your spouse keep your relationship thriving, you'll have a happier home, and your children will grow up in a healthy environment. So, go ahead. Plan a date with your spouse, and make a big deal about it. Leave little "countdown to our date" notes in your spouse's briefcase or vehicle. Act like you're 16 again, and let the romance begin . . .

KISSES FROM HEAVEN

Most important of all, continue to show deep love for each other . . .

1 Peter 4:8 (NLT)

HEART TO HEAVEN

Lord, thank You for my spouse. Help me to be the wife You've called me to be. Amen.

Chapter 4

GIFTS FROM GOD

School had just let out for the summer, and my girls were so excited! They had already made lots of plans to have friends over for swim parties, and they had volunteered me to play hostess with the mostest. Ally was already planning our first summer trip to the Fort Worth Zoo to see the new baby elephant, "Blue Bonnet." Of course, I wanted to do all of those things, but unfortunately, I was on a crazy tight book deadline and knew I wouldn't be able to give Abby and Ally my undivided attention for a couple of weeks. As I typed away at my desk in the sunroom, Ally ate peanut butter crackers while watching *Barney & Friends*, and Abby sat on the floor next to my desk, coloring pictures in her new art book. After typing the last word to the chapter I was working on, I noticed Ab, even closer to my desk now.

"What are you drawing?" I asked my artsy 7-year-old.

"Pictures of our family," she said, still coloring.

"Can I see it?" I asked in my fun Mommy voice.

Abby nodded and showed me her masterpiece. The picture featured Daddy playing a board game with her and Ally but I wasn't in the picture.

"That's very good, Ab," I encouraged. "But where am I?"

Without missing a beat, she flipped the page and said, "There you are, Mommy."

She had drawn me sitting at my desk, typing at my computer, all by myself.

That's when it hit me: *That's how she sees me.* I was the disconnected parent, on a different page in her life. I immediately shut down my computer, had a good cry, and promised God and my children that I would get my priorities in order. Thankfully, the girls were only 5 and 7 at the time when I got my wake-up call, so I didn't waste any more precious time. No matter my deadline, I made sure I had quality time with my babies every single day. If that meant I had to work very late after the rest of my family was in bed sometimes, that was just fine by me. (It was worth the sacrifice of sleep, though I lived on Diet Mountain Dew, Peanut M&Ms, and pure adrenaline some days.)

Now that my girls are 20 and 21, and Jeff and I are empty nesters, I would give anything for just one more summer with my girls at home. I'd give anything to host one more pool party. I long to load the girls into the SUV and head to the Fort Worth Zoo. But, those days are long gone. Time goes by far too quickly. One moment you're helping them pick out their clothes for preschool, and the next moment you're helping them choose their college. So, in case you are that disconnected parent on the different page in your child's life, let this serve as your wake-up call—WAKE UP! Time is precious and you don't want to lose it.

You don't have to spend lots of money to spend quality time with your children. Taking a walk around the block or playing a rousing game of Crazy Eights is totally free. So, make the most of those moments every summer and the rest of the year, as well. Because our children won't be around forever, and these are precious days—true gifts from God.

KISSES FROM HEAVEN

Teach us to number our days,
that we may gain a heart of wisdom.

Psalm 90:12 (NIV)

HEART TO HEAVEN

Lord, thank You for my children. Help me, Lord, to be a better time manager so that I can spend quality time with my family. And, help me, Father, to never lose sight of how precious they are to You and to me. I love You. Thank You for entrusting me with such precious children. In the mighty name of Jesus. Amen.

Chapter 5

WORTH THE WAIT

My sister Martie and I grew up in a home where we bought all of our produce. Mama never had a garden, so when my sister told me she had put out tomato plants last summer, I was quite impressed. Being a novice gardener, Martie researched exactly how far apart to space her tomato plants, what kind of fertilizer to use, how to keep away the destructive bugs, etc. Once they were planted, she tended to them daily, anxiously awaiting the juicy tomatoes to appear. But, day after day, her plants were tomato-less.

Frustrated, Martie gave in and went to the Saturday morning Farmer's Market in our hometown in search of fresh tomatoes. (I was there, too, but I was buying some homemade chocolate fudge two booths over. Wow, was it good!) While paying, Martie told the farmer her plight.

"I just don't get it," she said. "All of my neighbors who put out tomato plants the same time I did, all have tomatoes but I still don't have any."

The farmer paused to think for a moment and then asked, "Well, what kind of tomatoes did you plant?"

"You mean, there are different kinds?" Martie asked.

He nodded, and began rattling off a list of various kinds of tomatoes.

"I think they were called Big Boy," Martie remembered.

"Well there's your problem," the farmer explained. "Big Boy and Better Boy tomatoes have a 95-day gestation period whereas regular tomato plants produce fruit in as little as 70 days . . . you just have to wait a little longer for the Big Boys but they are my favorites."

With that new knowledge, Martie went home with renewed excitement over her upcoming Big Boy tomatoes, knowing they would be worth the wait.

Thinking about my sister's gardening experience, I had to smile. She just didn't know that Big Boy tomatoes took longer—neither did I—but once she discovered that information, she was no longer discouraged and upset about the lack of tomatoes on her plants. Instead, she was encouraged and excited to see them manifest a few weeks later.

Makes me wonder how many of us have "Big Boy" dreams in our hearts placed there by Almighty God, yet we just don't realize that they are of the "Big Boy" variety so we are discouraged and worn out with the waiting process. See, once we become moms, it seems that we often put our other dreams on hold. Maybe you've always felt God calling you to start your own business or write a book or get your master's degree, but you didn't think any of those things were possible while being a mother. Well, if God placed it on your heart to do those things, then He has already equipped you and will bring those dreams to fruition in His perfect timing. (I didn't write any of my more than 70 books until after I became a mom!) Turns out, I didn't have to choose between dreams—I could be a mother and a writer!

So, instead of thinking you have to give up on your other dreams because you're a mom, why not be encouraged today? Because if you're still waiting on your dreams to burst forth, that simply means that your dreams are more than likely "Big Boys," and they just take a little longer than regular dreams. They have a longer gestation period, but when God brings them forth, they will be better than you ever imagined and so worth the wait! So, the next time the devil tries to discourage you and tell you that your dreams are never coming to pass, say out loud: "My dreams are coming to pass in God's perfect timing. They are Big Boy dreams, and they are worth the wait!" And that, my friends is even better than homemade chocolate fudge!

KISSES FROM HEAVEN

Wait for the Lord; be strong, and let your heart take courage; wait for the Lord!

Psalm 27:14 (NRSV)

HEART TO HEAVEN

Lord, thank You for my Big Boy dreams. Help me to be patient during this gestation time, and help me to keep my eyes on You. In the mighty name of Jesus. Amen.

I LOVE YOU MORE THAN
A THOUSAND M&MS . . .

LOVING YOUR CHILDREN
UNCONDITIONALLY

MY FRIEND HEATHER SOWDERS NEW

I met Heather more than four years ago when my youngest daughter, Ally, started dating Heather's oldest son, Wesley. Ally not only fell in love with Wesley but also with his sweet family. They are some of the kindest, funniest, most loving, down-to-earth people you will ever meet, and they have been absolutely wonderful to my daughter.

And, unlike me, Wesley's mama can cook! In fact, she comes from a long line of accomplished cooks, so I was thrilled when she agreed to share one of her favorite chocolate recipes with us.

"As unconventional as it was, I grew up living with my grandmother, my dad's mom," Heather shared. "We never had much financially, but the fierce love for family was always felt and our bellies were always full of Mamaw's exceptional cooking.

"Because money was tight, each Christmas Mamaw would spend an entire day making fudge to give away to her nieces and nephews and church friends . . . Christmas without fudge . . . what's that?!"

What a wonderful family memory and tradition! In case you'd like to start that same "Family Fudge" tradition with your kin, here's that recipe.

MAMAW'S FUDGE

7-ounce jar of marshmallow cream

1 ½ cups white sugar

⅔ cup evaporated milk

¼ cup butter

¼ teaspoon salt

2 cups milk chocolate chips

1 cup semisweet chocolate chips

1 teaspoon vanilla

½ cup nuts

Line an 8x8 inch pan with aluminum foil, set aside. In a large saucepan over medium heat, combine marshmallow cream, sugar, evaporated milk, butter, and salt. Bring to a full boil and cook 5 minutes, stirring constantly. Remove from heat and pour in chocolate chips. Stir until melted and mixture is smooth. Stir in vanilla and nuts. Pour into pan, chill in refrigerator until firm (about 2 hours). Enjoy!

Chapter 6

LIVING THE LOVE CHAPTER

When I was a teenager, I drug myself into the kitchen every morning to grab a quick breakfast before school. I'd see my dad, sitting at the dining room table, glasses perched on his nose, reading his Bible. Dad started every day with black coffee, a package of little chocolate covered donuts, and the Word of God.

Years later, after being verbally attacked and belittled by another mother at the elementary school where our children attended, I stopped by my parents' home to lick my wounds and regroup before heading off to work. As I passed by the dining room, there sat my dad, in that familiar place.

In pure frustration, I plopped down next to him and sighed, stealing one of his chocolate donuts.

"Dad, how can you always be so nice to people—even people who are mean to you?"

"What happened?" he asked.

"This horrible woman actually threatened me because I put her daughter in the second act of the talent show," I explained. "What difference does it make? It's an elementary school talent show! Seriously?"

"So did you make the change?" he asked.

"Absolutely not! I will not be bullied into moving her daughter into the first act! If she thinks she can do a better job, then she should've volunteered to run the talent show instead of complaining about every decision I make."

I was just about to continue my rant when Dad gave me that fatherly look I'd seen a million times growing up.

"You think I should move her daughter to the first act, don't you?"

Then Dad said something I'll never forget.

"Honey, I've found that if you err on the side of love, you'll never have any regrets. Let me show you this . . . "

With that, Dad turned to a page marker in his Bible and read First Corinthians chapter 13—The Love Chapter—out loud. I could feel hot tears of conviction streaming down my face.

"I read this chapter every morning," he said, peering over the top of his reading glasses. "I've been doing that for many years. It'll change your life."

I knew he was right because I had seen my father walk in

love when others would have acted ugly, and I also knew that I needed more love in my life. I needed to be a better example of love to my children. I wanted to impact their lives with the love of Jesus the same way my dad had impacted my life.

I started that very day, reading The Love Chapter as part of my daily time with God. Sure I've missed a day or two over the years, but I've read it so many times that I now have it memorized. And, when I'm confronted with an angry stage mother or a rude salesperson or an agitated family member, I simply recite verses 4 through 8 until I can once again walk in love—just like my father and my Heavenly Father.

In case you don't have time to look up that passage right now, I thought I'd go ahead and provide it right here so you can begin reading it today.

Love is patient, love is kind. It does not envy, it does not boast, it is not proud. It does not dishonor others, it is not self-seeking, it is not easily angered, it keeps no record of wrongs. Love does not delight in evil but rejoices with the truth. It always protects, always trusts, always hopes, always perseveres. Love never fails.

Take it from my dad—it's always better to err on the side of love. Let's start living the love chapter in our daily lives, and let's start today.

KISSES FROM HEAVEN

Dear friends, let us continue to love one another,
for love comes from God. Anyone who loves
is a child of God and knows God.

1 John 4:7 (NLT)

HEART TO HEAVEN

Father, thank You for loving me unconditionally. Please fill me up with Your love so that I might walk in love day in and day out—no matter the circumstances—and impact my children's lives with Your love. In the mighty name of Jesus, Amen.

Chapter 7

WILL YOU ROCK ME?

"Twenty minus nine," Abby mumbled, tapping her pencil against the kitchen table.

"Eleven," I volunteered, while putting away the dinner dishes.

"Mom," Abby whined. "Don't help. I can do it myself!"

"Sorry," I said.

I was getting used to that response. At age 7, Abby's favorite expression was, "I can do it myself. I'm not a baby!" As much as it hurt me to hear those words, it was true. She dressed herself. She enjoyed styling her own hair. She could fix herself meals that didn't require the oven. She earned her own money by doing chores. She put away her own laundry. She was quite the independent little girl.

Later that night, as my husband Jeff, Allyson, and the two dogs slept in the den, Abby and I worked on her spelling words and drank chocolate milk (our favorite bedtime snack) in the living room. I relaxed in the recliner, watching Nick-at-Nite, while Abby finished writing her spelling words three times each. She wrote her last word just as "The Brady Bunch" ended and "I Love Lucy" came on.

"Time for bed," I said. "Make sure you brush your teeth."

"OK," she said. "I already laid out my clothes for tomorrow, but I need you to iron my shirt."

Minutes later, Abby returned to kiss me goodnight. After a quick peck on the cheek, she wandered part way down the hall and then came back.

"What's wrong, honey?" I asked, noticing she had a perplexed look on her face.

"Nothin'."

"I'll iron your shirt in a little while," I said, thinking that was the problem.

"That's not it," Abby said.

"Well, what is it?" I asked.

"Nothin'."

"Then you better get to bed. I'll be in to say prayers in a minute."

Abby gave me a hug and then she looked up at me with her big green eyes and whispered, "Mama, will you rock me?"

That's why she was acting so funny. It was hard for my little grown-up girl to admit she wanted her Mommy to rock her. I'm sure, in her mind, big girls didn't need to be rocked. Still, she found the courage to ask.

Her request brought tears to my eyes.

Ab fell asleep in my arms and I clung to her, wishing the moment would never end. Looking down at her as she slept, I thought about how much the Father loves us.

You know, after we've been Christians for a while, we tend to get very independent and self-sufficient. Like Abby, I long to "do it myself," and God allows me my independence—even if it means letting me calculate the answer "20 minus 9" and getting it wrong sometimes. He loves me enough to let me figure things out on my own.

But, don't you know that He loves it when we swallow our pride, crawl up in His lap, and whisper, "Father, will You rock me?" Don't you imagine that it thrills Him as much as it thrilled me when Abby asked me that question?

God is a parent, and He enjoys loving His children. It says in the Bible that we can come boldly into His throne room. Do you know why? Because He is our Dad, and what kind of dad would deny his children access to him? He just wants to be with us, nurture us, and love us. He gave His Son Jesus to die on the cross so that we could be in fellowship with Him for eternity.

Now that's love.

So, why not take advantage of your rights as a covenant

child of God? Go ahead. Crawl up in your Heavenly Father's lap today and let Him love you a while. He's got a recliner in the throne room, and his lap is always available to you.

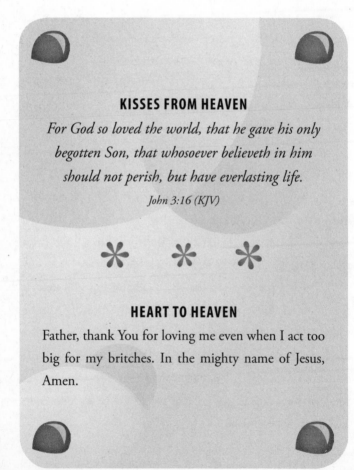

KISSES FROM HEAVEN

For God so loved the world, that he gave his only begotten Son, that whosoever believeth in him should not perish, but have everlasting life.

John 3:16 (KJV)

HEART TO HEAVEN

Father, thank You for loving me even when I act too big for my britches. In the mighty name of Jesus, Amen.

Chapter 8

LOVE YOU MORE

"I love you a million red M&Ms."

That's one of my favorite lines from the movie *What a Girl Wants*, starring Amanda Bynes as Daphne Reynolds and Kelly Preston as her mom, Libby Reynolds. *What a Girl Wants* is one of the movies that the girls grew up watching, and we probably watched it once a week for years! Believe me when I tell you, I know this movie line by line. Just last week, I was flipping through the channels before bedtime, and there it was! I hadn't seen that movie in many years! It was like an old friend stopped by to say hello via my TV screen. I not only watched it, I DVR'd it so I could watch it again later. (Told you I loved it!)

In one of the opening scenes, Daphne is sad that the father she's never known, except through pictures and the stories her mom has told her, isn't present for yet another birthday. Noticing how sad her daughter is on a day that's supposed to be very happy, Libby says, "I love you a million Swedish Fish." And, without missing a beat, Daphne responds, "I love you a million red M&Ms."

Doesn't that just melt your heart?

Not only is it a precious mother/daughter moment, but it involves chocolate! Their tender exchange inspired Abby, Ally, and me to come up with our own "Love you more thans . . ." over the years.

Here are our top five:

1. I love you more than a giant Hershey Kiss.
2. I love you more than the fluffiest pillow.
3. I love you more than McDonald's french fries.
4. I love you more than a shopping spree with no spending limit.
5. I love you more than a Sno-cone with extra flavoring.

This is such a fun game to play on road trips. (It's especially effective to stopping petty fights in the backseat, as well as discontinuing comments such as, "Mom, she's touching me!") Always worked for us. Also, it's a great way to say, "I love you" in a non-mushy, kid-friendly way so if your kiddos are going through that stage where pretty much everything embarrasses them—especially affection-showing parents—saying "I love you more than a giant Hershey Kiss" is less horrifying for them.

More than anything, making up new ways to say "I love you" is a great way to encourage loving relationships in your household. Maybe you grew up in a home where "I love you" wasn't said on a regular basis, or maybe not at all. If that's the case, saying "I love you" might not come as easily to you, even though you show your love by all the things you do for your family. Still, children need to hear that they are loved.

I recently read an article about this very topic on a website called "The Mother Company." In this piece, Dr. Christine Carter, a sociologist and happiness expert at UC Berkeley's The Greater Good Science Center, said it is very important for children to hear "I love you."

"Obviously, love and affection are the most important things for our children," she explained. "There's plenty of research out there saying that those two things affect their outcomes, emotional well-being, and academic achievement. The words are important—the expression of our emotions amplify our loving actions."

So, find lots of new ways to say you love your children today. Then, have each child come up with a new way to express love to our Heavenly Father. There's nothing quite like a day of love.

KISSES FROM HEAVEN

I have loved you with an everlasting love.

Jeremiah 31:3 (NIV)

HEART TO HEAVEN

Lord, thank You for loving me unconditionally. Help me to express my love to my children and let them know how much they are cherished and treasured. Help me to love my family the same way that You love me. I love You, God, and I am so thankful for who You are and all that You've done in my life. In the mighty name of Jesus, Amen.

Chapter 9

UNDER HIS COVERING

"Mommy, hurry!" Abby, my then 7-year-old called from the middle of the driveway. "It's a baby bird!"

Sure enough, right in the middle of our driveway lay a sweet, fluffy, baby dove. He had all of his feathers, but the dainty dove still couldn't fly. He had obviously fallen from a nest in the large live oak tree a few feet away. I didn't know what to do, so I called the Texas Wildlife Headquarters.

After explaining our bird situation, the nice man on the other end of the line told me exactly how to handle our dove dilemma in order to save our new feathered friend.

"So I need to make a makeshift nest and put it into a hanging basket, and then place that basket near the tree?" I repeated back. "OK, will do. Thanks for all of your help."

I hung up the phone and rushed to the front door to check on the baby bird before heading to the garage to construct a makeshift nest, and that's when I saw one of the most beautiful sights I'd ever seen—the mother dove nuzzling her baby bird—right in the middle of our driveway. She was protecting her baby at all costs. As I watched the mama dove be so tender with her fallen baby bird, spreading her wings and wrapping them around him, I thought, "All moms are alike. We'd risk our lives for the sake of our children's lives. We'd protect them at all costs. We devote our lives to sheltering our babies from harm, nourishing and caring for them, and raising them to be strong enough to fly."

In that moment, I realized why God had chosen that same image to describe his love for us: "He will cover you with his feathers. He will shelter you with his wings . . . " (Psalm 91:4, NLT). God loves us and our children more than we can ever fathom. He adores us! He cares about each one of us. When we fall out of our respective nests, He is right there, hovering over us, protecting us, and loving us until we're out of harm's way. That's just who He is, and I'm so thankful, aren't you?

Using the fallen dove in our driveway as a teachable moment, I quietly showed my girls how the mother dove was with her baby bird and protecting him no matter what.

"That mama dove and baby bird are just like us," I continued. "I would protect you at all costs. I love you more than you can ever imagine, and I only want the very best for you."

Abby hugged my legs, while my then 5-year-old Ally continued munching on M&Ms.

"And you know what else?" I asked. "God loves you both even more than I do, and that's an awful lot, and He will always be there to watch over you and protect you even when Mommy can't."

Abby hugged me even tighter. Ally popped another M&M into her mouth.

"Now let's go build that nest for the baby bird," I said, feeling quite happy about the tender moment we'd just shared.

Abby headed for the garage, but Ally headed toward the baby bird.

"Where are you going, Ally?"

"To share my M&Ms with the baby bird," she answered, matter-of-factly. "You said we were just like the birds, and I like M&Ms."

I could see there would need to be more teachable moments in our very near future . . .

KISSES FROM HEAVEN

Look at the birds of the air; they do not sow or reap or store away in barns, and yet your heavenly Father feeds them. Are you not much more valuable than they?

Matthew 6:26 (NIV)

HEART TO HEAVEN

Father, thank You, for always being there for me—protecting and loving me no matter what. I pray that You'll help me watch over my little birds the same way that You care for me. In the mighty name of Jesus. Amen.

Chapter 10

IT'S WHAT'S ON THE INSIDE . . .

I've often joked that I've never met a piece of chocolate I didn't like, but that's not actually true. When I first moved to Texas, I was at a store in the Fort Worth Stockyards, and a cowboy who worked there offered me a sample.

"I never turn down chocolate," I said, smiling. "What kind is it?"

"It's one of our famous truffles," he said in his very southern drawl. "You're not from around here, are you?"

"Well, not originally," I explained. "We just moved here from Indiana . . . Oh, I love truffles."

Just as I bit into it, he added: "But I bet you've never had a chipotle truffle before."

He was right.

I hadn't.

It was the hottest piece of chocolate I'd ever eaten, and it was just—wrong!

I somehow managed to swallow it and said, "Sir, chocolate is supposed to be sweet, not hot!"

Without missing a beat, he said, "Well, you're in Texas now. We like everything hot."

Needless to say, I didn't buy any of their "World famous Chipotle Truffles." Instead, I headed for the nearest place I could get a Diet Coke so I could wash that awful flavor out of my mouth.

That experience was a good reminder for me—just because it looks like every other truffle you've ever eaten doesn't mean it's going to taste like them. It's what is on the inside that makes a truffle sweet or, in this case, spicy. And, it's the same with us. We may all appear basically alike on the outside, but it's what is on the inside that really matters. That's why the Scriptures say that man looks on the outward appearance, but God looks at our hearts.

And, since we're supposed to be like Jesus, we should strive to do that with our loved ones—especially our children. Even though it's difficult at times, we need to look past the outer stuff and focus on the heart of the matter.

I've found that shift in thinking makes a world of difference.

For example, Abby, who was 9 at the time, had been coming home from school very grumpy for several weeks, fighting with her sister and complaining nonstop. It wasn't like her, so I knew something was up. After prodding and praying for discernment, I discovered that Abby was having trouble reading and was falling behind in class. This caused my little Type A personality to be embarrassed and very stressed. Through testing, we learned that Abby suffered from light sensitivity which adversely affected her reading, yet was very treatable. By simply putting a lavender-colored screen over her reading assignments, all was right with the world again.

But what if I hadn't looked for the deeper issue? What if I had just looked at her "spicy" behavior, disciplined her for that, and hadn't gone to the heart of the matter? We might never have learned of that light sensitivity issue, which could've negatively affected the rest of her years of schooling.

So, here's what I'm asking you to do this week. When one of your children is having a "spicy" moment, before you unleash "Disciplinarian Mom," take a moment to see the heart of the matter. What's going on inside your child that is causing the "spicy" behavior? Sometimes it's simply because your little angel is tired or hungry or not feeling well. All of those physical conditions can cause "spicy" moments. But, sometimes it's something much deeper, and often we discipline our kids for their "spicy behavior" without ever finding out the deeper issue going on inside their little hearts.

I'm all for discipline, setting boundaries, and raising well-behaved children, but I'm also for championing our children. As moms, that's what we do best.

KISSES FROM HEAVEN

To discipline a child produces wisdom, but a mother is disgraced by an undisciplined child.

Proverbs 29:15 (NLT)

HEART TO HEAVEN

Father, thank You for my children. Help me to look past their "spicy" outward behavior and focus in on the heart of the matter so that I can take action accordingly. I am asking for Your guidance and discernment, Lord. In the mighty name of Jesus. Amen.

LETTING GO, LETTING GOD, GETTING GODIVA . . .

LEARNING TO GIVE YOUR CHILDREN TO GOD

MY MOTHER-IN-LAW MARTHA DAVIS

My mother-in-law, otherwise known as Nana, rarely comes over without bringing us a special treat. From her persimmon pudding to her chocolate chip cookies to her milk chocolate brownies—we never go hungry when Nana is around. At 81, Nana still works full-time and often treats her co-workers to some of her baked goodies, as well.

Though everything she fixes is amazing, my daughters love Nana's brownies the very best, so that's what I asked Nana to contribute to this book. Paired with an ice cold glass of milk—it just doesn't get any better than that!

NANA'S BROWNIES

¾ cup flour

¼ teaspoon salt

¼ teaspoon baking soda

⅓ cup butter

2 tablespoons milk

¾ cup sugar

2 cups milk chocolate chips, divided

2 eggs

1 teaspoon vanilla

1 cup chopped, toasted walnuts (optional)

Combine flour, salt, and baking soda, and set aside. Melt the butter, milk, and sugar over medium low heat, stirring continuously. When the mixture is just ready to boil, remove from heat and immediately stir in 1 cup of the milk chocolate chips. Next, pour the chocolate mixture into a large mixing bowl and add the eggs, one at a time. Then add the vanilla, and gradually add the flour mixture. After blending well, add the remaining chocolate chips and nuts. Pour batter into a greased 9×9 pan, and bake for 30 to 35 minutes at 325°. (Nana's tip—don't overbake!)

Chapter 11

GOD STILL DOES MIRACLES

When I was only 11 weeks pregnant with our second baby, I was leaving the YMCA after teaching a low-impact aerobics class when I doubled over with pain in the parking lot. I knew something was wrong.

I drove straight to my OBGYN and through tears explained what was going on. After an exam and what seemed like hours, the doctor said very matter-of-factly, "I'm afraid I don't have good news—you're experiencing a miscarriage. I want you to go home and rest with your feet up, and if you pass it before Monday, go to the ER."

"That's it? There's nothing else you can do?"

"I'm afraid not," he said, patting me on the back.

Lying on our couch with my feet up, per doctor's orders, I couldn't help but think, *This can't be it. This can't be the end of the story.*

"Sis!" my older sister Martie called, making her way through the house. "Mom just told me."

Martie listened to me relay the horrible diagnosis, and then she said, "Get up and get ready. You're coming with us to church."

"Did you not just hear what the doctor said I had to do?"

"Yes I heard," she continued. "But I know you and Jeff are supposed to go with us to hear this evangelist tonight."

Knowing my sister would never take "no" for an answer, my parents, my sister and her husband, and Jeff and I went to a revival service to hear an evangelist I knew nothing about in a place I'd never been before.

I tried to listen as he preached, but I kept thinking about my baby. I looked down at my belly that wasn't showing with pregnancy yet, and wondered if this miscarriage was my fault for teaching low-impact aerobics. Just then, the evangelist stopped his message, got very quiet, and said, "Someone here has been told that you are going to miscarry your baby today, and I'm here to tell you that's a lie from the pit of hell. Come up here, I want to pray for you."

I froze—unable to move at all—wondering if he was talking about me or if possibly another woman could have received my same dismal diagnosis. Another lady across the auditorium stood up, and he said to her, "Ma'am you're not the one God showed me, but I will pray for you . . . "

Before I could think another thought, the evangelist walked all the way to the back, grabbed my hand, and led me down front. Hot tears filled my eyes and my throat. That evangelist pointed right at my belly and said, "I declare today that your little girl will live and not die and declare the works of the Lord! And you will not have any more trouble with this pregnancy!"

As soon as he spoke those words, I felt an intense warmth flow through my body. It was so overwhelming that I fell to the ground—actually on top of the evangelist, I later learned. The next half hour is a blur for me, but I remember lying on the ground, knowing that God had restored my pregnancy, knowing that I was having a baby girl, and knowing that she would be mighty for God.

Monday's doctor's appointment confirmed what I already knew—there was a strong heartbeat, and it belonged to my baby girl. Allyson Michelle Adams was born on Aug. 15, 1994. As she turned 20 this year, I reminded her that God used her very birth to lead our family into a deeper faith and that He has a very big call on her life.

She's my miracle.

So, fellow Mama, if you're believing God for a miracle today, be encouraged! We serve a God who makes a way where there is no way. And, He is still in the miracle-working business—just ask Ally.

KISSES FROM HEAVEN

You are the God who performs miracles;
you display your power among the peoples.

Psalm 77:14 (NIV)

HEART TO HEAVEN

Lord, help me to believe. Thank You, God, for doing the impossible in my life. In the mighty name of Jesus, Amen.

Chapter 12

PRAYER WORKS!

I normally start my day with prayer, but I was running late for my sister's Bible study that particular morning, so I skipped my prayer time, grabbed a chocolate breakfast bar and a Diet Coke, and hurried out the door. Just as I was pulling out of the driveway, I felt a real urgency to pray for my daughters. With the three-hour time difference between Indiana and California, I knew Ally wasn't even up yet, but Abby was already headed to Kentucky to see her boyfriend pitch in a college baseball tournament. I prayed Psalm 91 over Ally and Abby and thanked God that their guardian angels were watching over them. I continued praying and praising God for my precious daughters until I felt a peace come over me. Then I went ahead into Bible study, walking in only a few minutes late.

Moments later, my phone vibrated. Just as I was about to turn off my phone, I saw the call was from Abby so I excused myself and answered.

"Mom," she said, through sobs.

"What's wrong?"

"I was just almost in an accident . . . "

After hearing those words, my heart was pounding so hard that I thought it would escape my chest. Abby went on to explain what had happened to her.

A car pulled out of the median, almost side-swiping her, causing her to swerve into the right lane to avoid contact. Before the incident was over, her car and three others were off the road, and Abby's vehicle had spun completely around.

"Mom, I don't even know how that car missed me," she kept saying. "I saw it coming right at me!"

I knew.

"Because at the exact time this happened to you, Ab, God prompted me to pray for you," I shared. "I was praying Psalm 91 over you and thanking God that your guardian angels were watching over you this morning!"

We both cried and praised the Lord and rejoiced that this was only an "almost accident" and such a powerful lesson for both of us. She was amazed and touched that God cared so much for her that He would have me pray at the exact time she would be encountering what could have been a terrible accident. And, I was so thankful that God had prompted me to pray especially since I had been negligent to pray earlier that morning, and that I had recognized His voice and been obedient to do so.

Abby and I thought about that incident for several days following. We both knew it had been divine intervention, and it had increased our faith.

People who aren't Christians might write this off as "a mother's intuition," but we know better. It was God who caused me to pray at the exact time that Abby was coming up on that crazy driver, and it was God who miraculously moved her car out of harm's way.

As mothers, we are that first line of prayer defense when it comes to our kiddos. With everything we do for our children—from being their taxi drivers to fixing their meals to doing their laundry to helping them with homework—nothing is more important than covering them with prayer. This incident with Abby reminded me just how important my prayers are for my children, and I hope this devotion serves as a reminder for you, too.

If you need help knowing what to pray for your children, there are books with prayer helps such as Stormie Omartian's *The Power of a Praying Parent* and *The Power of Praying for Your Adult Children*. Also, I find it's helpful to keep a prayer journal, recording when and what I prayed for my girls. It's exciting to look back through my prayer journal and rejoice over all the answered prayers!

So, go ahead. Get your prayer on! It's not only our job; it's our greatest privilege.

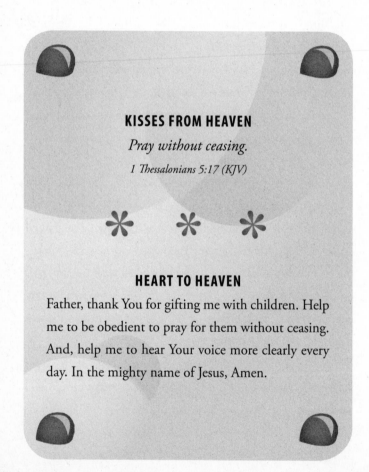

KISSES FROM HEAVEN

Pray without ceasing.

1 Thessalonians 5:17 (KJV)

* * *

HEART TO HEAVEN

Father, thank You for gifting me with children. Help me to be obedient to pray for them without ceasing. And, help me to hear Your voice more clearly every day. In the mighty name of Jesus, Amen.

Chapter 13

DO YOU TRUST ME?

It was a dark and rainy night as I drove home from a nearby city. My then 3-year-old daughter Abby lay asleep in her car seat next to me. Because of the bad weather, I decided to bypass the usual way and take a different, more lighted road home. Just as I whipped our Ford Explorer in a different direction, Abby awoke.

"We're lost aren't we, Mommy?" she asked, rubbing her eyes.

"No, honey. Mommy's just taking a different route home tonight."

I could see the doubt in Abby's eyes as headlights from a passing car illuminated our vehicle.

After a few more minutes, she said, "I don't think this is the right way."

"Ab, do you trust me enough to try it *my* way?"

As I uttered those words, conviction covered me like a heavy blanket. The Holy Spirit reminded me how I'd questioned God earlier that week. I knew in my heart that I was supposed to wait for the freelance writing job God had promised me, but a good full-time journalistic opportunity was dangling in front of me. I wasn't sure whether or not to take that full-time job and hope that God would bless it anyway, or wait for the freelance job that had been such a long time coming.

Maybe God had changed His mind, I'd reasoned earlier that week.

So that night, I cried out: "God, what's going on? The freelance job that I felt you had for me doesn't appear to be any closer to being mine than it was six months ago. Do you really think I should let this full-time writing opportunity pass me by? You know, we're really hurting for money right now. What if I turn down this job and the other one never comes my way?"

Just then, I heard my Heavenly Father say—not audibly but in that still, small voice: "Michelle, do you trust Me enough to try it My way?"

Tears streamed down my face, keeping time with the raindrops on the windshield. I thanked God for being so patient with my fledgling faith.

The following day, I turned down the full-time job that

offered an immediate solution to our financial situation, trusting God to perform His Word. And, He did—just like He'd promised. Two weeks later, that steady freelance opportunity was mine, and it paid even more than I had expected! I celebrated with chocolate-covered peanuts, and praised God for His faithfulness.

You see, God always does more than we could ask or think if we'll only trust in Him. Some days I'm better at doing that than others, but I'm learning that God's ways are always better than mine (Isaiah 55:8). We can trust Him with our careers, our hopes, our finances, and our children. I've discovered that God's ways aren't always the easiest, and sometimes they don't even make sense to me, but He only asks us to follow Him. He doesn't ask us to figure it out first, and then follow Him.

Just like I had asked Abby to trust me, God wants us to trust Him. Are you willing to trust Him enough to do things His way? If you'll relinquish that control, you'll discover that our Heavenly Father really does know best.

KISSES FROM HEAVEN

Trust in the Lord with all your heart,
And lean not on your own understanding;
In all your ways acknowledge Him,
And He shall direct your paths.

Proverbs 3:5-6 (NKJV)

HEART TO HEAVEN

Father, help me to trust You more and follow You without hesitation. I know that You have the best for me, but I often try to work things out on my own, thinking I can handle it. I admit today that I can't handle it, God, and I submit all of my heart, my hopes, my dreams, my family and my life to You. I love You. In the mighty name of Your Son, Jesus, Amen.

Chapter 14

DO YOU KNOW HIS VOICE?

I've always loved Doris Day, and so have my girls. You see, on rainy days, my daughters and I would make smores, put on our favorite jammies, and have classic movie marathons on my big bed. Sometimes my husband Jeffrey even joined us.

On one such rainy afternoon, we enjoyed a Doris Day/James Garner double feature: *The Thrill of It All* and *Move Over, Darling*. As the second movie ended, Abby and Allyson retreated to their playroom for some serious playtime before "lights out."

Because it was a weekend, Jeff and I agreed to let the girls sleep in the playroom so they could fall asleep watching a movie. Before I knew it, the hour was 11 p.m. I crawled into bed and drifted off to sleep.

After only a few zzzs, I felt hot breath on my cheek.

I opened one eye to see Abby standing right over me.

"What's wrong, Ab?" I mumbled.

"I just heard Doris Day at the end of that movie we rented," Abby whispered with much excitement. "She's singing some song about trouble tree plants and tight ropes.

Trouble tree plants and tight ropes, I pondered. *Hmmmm.*

"Oh, you mean, rubber tree plants and high hopes!" I said, quite pleased with myself for figuring out that one.

"Yeah, that's it," she beamed. "C'mon Mommy, you've got to hear it."

So, I rolled out of bed, stumbled down the hallway, and poked my head into the playroom long enough to hear Doris Day's beautiful voice singing "High Hopes."

"Yep, that's her!" I assured Abby. "Good ear. I can't believe you knew it was her without even seeing her."

"I know her voice," Abby said quite proudly.

Later, as I was trying to fall back asleep, I thought about what Abby had said: "I know her voice."

At the time, Abby was only 6 years old, yet I had exposed her to so many Doris Day movies that it took her only seconds to identify Miss Day's voice. She knew it was Doris without even seeing her. I smiled, realizing I had raised a serious Doris Day fan. But then I thought of something else that didn't make me smile.

I wondered, *have I exposed my girls to God's Word enough that they would know His voice that quickly?*

Sure, I had taken them to church from the time they were born, but had I talked about His Word and His blessings as enthusiastically as I had talked about Doris Day's career and her movie credits? Could Abby recite Scriptures as well as she could recite the words to "The Thrill of it All"?

I wasn't sure.

I realized that I needed to spend more time encouraging my girls in the Word of God.

After that night, I didn't refer to my devotion time as a "have to" obligation anymore. Instead, I let the girls know that Mommy was retreating to her room to have an exciting conversation with the Lord. And I no longer found excuses to get out of going to Wednesday night church services. Instead, I'd pick up the girls from school on Wednesdays and start talking about how much fun we were going to have that night at church.

Lastly, we started piling onto Abby's bed every night and reading from a children's devotional book. Then, we'd all join hands and pray together. That special time became another family tradition in our home.

Today I am happy to report that my girls have come to know God's voice just as well as they know Doris Day's.

Knowing that has given me "High Hopes" for my daughters' futures. So I ask you: How well do you know God's voice? How well do your children know His voice?

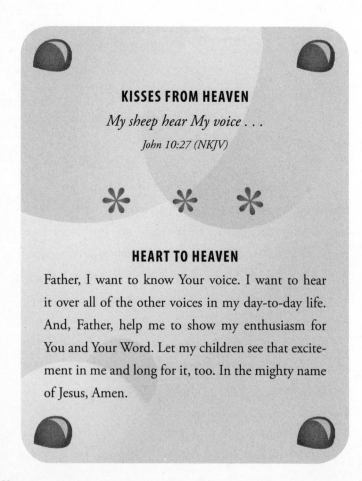

KISSES FROM HEAVEN

My sheep hear My voice . . .
John 10:27 (NKJV)

* * *

HEART TO HEAVEN

Father, I want to know Your voice. I want to hear it over all of the other voices in my day-to-day life. And, Father, help me to show my enthusiasm for You and Your Word. Let my children see that excitement in me and long for it, too. In the mighty name of Jesus, Amen.

LETTING THE CHOCOLATE CHIPS FALL WHERE THEY MAY . . .

NEVER SWEATING THE SMALL STUFF

MY AUNT BETTY PERRY CHASE

If there's one thing that I remember about my Aunt Betty, it's this—that lady could cook! In fact, her Mississippi Mud Cake was so good that people all over our hometown requested her recipe. Now this was before the days of easy access to copy machines, so my kind aunt would have to write out the lengthy recipe by hand every time she got a request. Of course, some of the smarter people in town cut right to the chase and simply asked her to bake the cake for them. One such gentleman was an attorney in town. She made him a Mississippi Mud Cake every year, and to show his appreciation, he had his secretary type up the recipe and make copies so Aunt Betty wouldn't have to handwrite it every single time she had a new request.

AUNT BETTY'S
MISSISSIPPI MUD CAKE

4 eggs

2 cups sugar

1 cup shortening

1 teaspoon vanilla

1 cup nuts such as pecans

7 ounce jar of marshmallow cream

1 can or ½ cup of shredded sweetened coconut

1 ½ cups flour

½ cup cocoa

¼ teaspoon salt

Mix shortening and sugar until creamy. Add eggs and sift in flour, salt, and cocoa. Add vanilla and nuts.

Bake at 350° for 30 minutes. Remove from oven and spread marshmallow cream and coconut and return to oven for 3 minutes to melt.

Icing:

2 sticks margarine

⅕ can condensed milk

⅓ cup cocoa

1 box of powdered sugar

1 teaspoon vanilla

Combine sugar and cocoa, and then add melted margarine, milk, and vanilla. Lastly, spread icing onto the cooled cake.

Chapter 15

IT'S A DOG-EAT-DOG WORLD

"Allyson, let's go, honey!" I called to my then 4-year-old daughter.

As we rounded the corner, I noticed a sign on the bulletin board: "Dress like the family member you most admire this Friday."

"That's *tomorrow!*" I mumbled to myself, already planning to turn Allyson into a mini me.

She could carry a briefcase, I thought. *And, I could pull her hair into a professional-looking clip.*

As I loaded Allyson into our SUV, I said, "Ally, I read where you are supposed to dress up tomorrow like someone in your family that you admire. Are you going to do it?"

"Yep," she said.

"So, *who* are you going to dress up like?" I smugly asked.

Allyson looked up at me with her big blue eyes and sweetly said, "Maddie."

"MADDIE!" I shrieked. "But you can't dress up like our *dog!*"

Well, I thought, *I'll be a laughing stock. I bet nobody else's daughter dresses up like the family dog! Doesn't she know I have stretch marks because of her? I've earned the right to be the "Most Admired Person" in her life.*

Once home, Allyson breezed past me on her way to see the popular Maddie—our miniature dachshund with an attitude twice her size.

As soon as I heard Allyson's giggles and Maddie's barks, I sighed. Maddie, the little furball, had won. I'd lost the title of "Most Admired" to a wiener dog.

There was nothing left to do except make the costume. Fueled by Diet Mountain Dew and a handful of Peanut M&Ms, I started working on the Maddie ensemble. At about 11:30 p.m., I finished the best dog costume ever created and called it a night.

"Hold still," I coached, applying black makeup to Allyson's nose. When I'd finished, she stepped in front of the mirror and gave her best "Bark" before heading off to preschool.

On the drive there, I kept glancing at Allyson in the rearview mirror. She looked so cute and so pleased with herself. I, on the other hand, was mortified.

How could I lose to a dog? I thought.

As we pulled in, I noticed all of the other little girls were dressed like their mothers—all but my daughter. I swallowed hard and walked Allyson to the door.

As we passed a group of mommies, one of them asked, "And who are you supposed to be, honey?"

"I'm Maddie," Allyson said, smiling. "She's my dog."

The woman snickered, and the other mommies chimed in with chortles.

"Well, you are a very beautiful dog," the woman added.

Then Allyson said something I'll cherish forever.

"Thank you," she said. "My mommy made my costume because she's the bestest mommy in the whole world."

With that, Allyson kissed me goodbye, leaving a black smudge on my face and a warm feeling in my heart.

OK, so I lost out to a wiener dog, but I really won. Not only did I learn to love my daughter no matter what, but also I learned to choose my battles very carefully.

Sure I could have insisted that Allyson dress up like a miniature me, but she wanted desperately to dress up like her precious puppy. By partnering with Allyson to accomplish her desire, I let her know that I would support her and love her unconditionally, even when she didn't choose me first— much like the Heavenly Father loves me when I don't choose

Him first. Yes, there were many lessons to be learned from that one event. It caused me to step off the Pride Path and onto Unconditional Love Lane, and I've been trying to walk in love ever since.

Why not join me on the journey? Don't let every little thing become a big battle. Instead, look for little opportunities to show your child big love today.

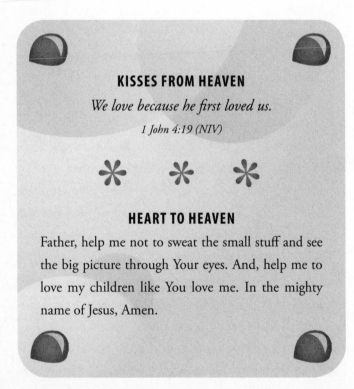

KISSES FROM HEAVEN

We love because he first loved us.
1 John 4:19 (NIV)

* * *

HEART TO HEAVEN

Father, help me not to sweat the small stuff and see the big picture through Your eyes. And, help me to love my children like You love me. In the mighty name of Jesus, Amen.

Chapter 16

CELEBRATE EVERY MOMENT

One of the movies I watch over and over again is *Just Married,* starring Ashton Kutcher and Brittany Murphy. Maybe you've seen it. The movie is about a young couple who falls hard and fast for each other, gets married, and has the worst honeymoon ever—accidentally burning down a castle in Europe, sleeping in their rental car in a blizzard, and even getting arrested! They are so angry with each other and so disappointed at how their dream honeymoon turns out, they decide to divorce upon their return home.

Very sad about the demise of his marriage, Ashton's character, Tom Leezak, visits with his dad for some fatherly advice. The conversation goes like this:

"Gonna tell me what you're chewing on?" Mr. Leezak asks.

"I just don't know if love is enough anymore," Tom replies. "I mean, even if Sarah and I do love each other . . . maybe we did need more time to get to know each other."

"So, what you're saying here is . . . you had a couple of bad days in Europe, and it's over?" Mr. Leezak asks. "Time to grow up, Tommy. Some days your mother and I loved each other. Other days we had to work at it. You never see the hard days in a photo album, but those are the ones that get you from one happy snapshot to the next."

I love that line because it's so true. Every day of motherhood—or life for that matter—isn't all triple-dipped milk chocolate covered peanuts and dark chocolate truffles. But, looking through photographs from past vacations, honor days, field trips, sporting events, family reunions, birthday parties, holidays, and other life events, you'd think every day of motherhood was happy, fun, and amazing. Why? Because those photo albums feature happy, smiling, laughing, hugging, and sometimes downright goofy pictures of your family. You rarely see photos of people crying, depressed, or angry in photo albums or posted on someone's Facebook page. No, even most of the candid shots usually ooze happiness. How many times have you pointed a camera at your kiddos and said, "Say cheese" and snapped the cheesiest smiles ever? We rarely point our cameras at our children when they are having a tantrum on the floor or crying over a recent heartbreak, do we?

Of course not.

In reality, life isn't always so happy. It isn't always so full of "Kodak moments." On the day when your child isn't chosen for the cheer squad or your son doesn't get into his college of choice, or your baby is bullied at school, you have to hold onto the happy memories and stand strong on the Word of God to make it through until the next Kodak moment comes along. We need to live each day mindful that every moment is precious. And, we need to thank God for all of the Kodak moments and even for the ones in between because those "in between moments" are often when we grow, learn, and become more appreciative of those snapshot-worthy moments in life. No matter what kind of day it is, we need to say, "This is the day the Lord has made; I will rejoice and be glad in it." With that kind of attitude, even the less-than-picture-perfect moments will be ones you'll treasure.

KISSES FROM HEAVEN

This is the day which the Lord has made;
let us rejoice and be glad in it.

Psalm 118:24 (NASB)

HEART TO HEAVEN

Father, thank You for filling my life with family, and thank You for all of the Kodak moments I've already experienced and for the ones still in my future. Help me to never take any of it for granted, and help me to teach my children to do the same. I love You, God, and I am so thankful for another day to live and love. In the mighty name of Jesus, Amen.

Chapter 17

WAL-MART WISDOM

As we strolled through Wal-Mart, my then 3-year-old Abby found a panda bear stuffed animal that she just couldn't live without. She grabbed it and hugged it and danced around the aisle as if it were her new best friend. Ally, who always imitated everything her older sister did, grabbed a stuffed elephant and did the same happy dance in time with Abby.

"Abby, honey, it's too close to your birthday to be buying random toys," I explained. "Now put the panda bear back, and you might get it for your birthday or possibly Christmas . . . that goes for you, too, Ally."

Now, normally, Abby was the reasonable one, but she really wanted this panda bear, and she simply wasn't taking no for an answer.

Totally ignoring my request to put the bear back, Abby clung to the furry panda and began crying, "Please, Mommy! Please, I want it real bad!"

"Not today," I said, a bit more firmly.

With that, Abby threw herself on the floor and proceeded to have "the mother of all meltdowns." Ally, who was almost two at the time, let out some sympathy cries, adding to the scene.

Trying to gain control of the situation, I grabbed the panda bear and the elephant and tried to place them back onto the rounder of plush toys, but Abby wasn't giving up so easily. She wouldn't let go of the panda, and somehow ended up falling backwards into the stuffed animal display, scattering stuffed toys in every direction.

It was quite a scene. And, of course, pretty much everyone I knew happened to be shopping at Wal-Mart that day. I kept waiting for Wal-Mart security to come and kick us out of the store, but instead an elderly gentleman from church stopped by to lend a helping hand. As we picked up the last of the stuffed toys and placed them on the rounder, he smiled and patted me on the back.

Looking at my daughters, who were now hiding behind the shopping cart, knowing they were in big trouble, he said "They are so precious. These are the best years of your life. Treasure every moment."

As he walked off toward frozen foods, I stood there bewildered.

Had he not just witnessed the meltdown of all meltdowns, with the subsequent stuffed toy explosion? I remember thinking, *If these are the best days of my life, I hope Jesus comes back for us today.*

That's been more than 17 years ago, but his words have stayed with me. Those were precious years. I can see that now. Sometimes, when you're smack dab in the middle of all the craziness, you can't see it. So, if you're a mom to preschoolers—take some advice from the wise old man at my church—treasure each moment. Those years are gone too quickly, and while every phase of their growing up is special, there's something pretty wonderful about those early years of sticky kisses, uncontrollable giggles, and even the occasional meltdown.

I'm glad that old man shared that truth with me that day. I call it "Wal-Mart Wisdom." It was priceless to me and has served me well over the years. I hope it does the same for you.

But, even if your children are no longer preschoolers, it's not too late. Take time today to love your babies—no matter how old they are. If they still fit on your lap, spend time reading together or curling up and watching a movie. If they are a little older, why not bake some chocolate fudge brownies together? Or, if they are like my kiddos and away at college, or perhaps in the military, send a text today and simply say, "I love you and miss you, but I am so proud of the person you've become. Can't wait to see you again!" Let's treasure our children today and every day!

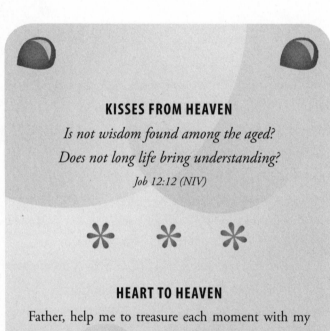

KISSES FROM HEAVEN

Is not wisdom found among the aged?
Does not long life bring understanding?
Job 12:12 (NIV)

✳   ✳   ✳

HEART TO HEAVEN

Father, help me to treasure each moment with my children and not wish my life away, longing for what's ahead. In the mighty name of Jesus, Amen.

Chapter 18

BREAKING THE MOTHER'S CURSE

It's been called, "The Mother's Curse."

"I hope you have a child that is just like you when you grow up!"

Chances are, your own mother has uttered those words to you, usually following something you did that totally aggravated her. And, chances are—you did have a child just like you! In my case, I had two. You know what's interesting about raising children that are exactly like you? You tend to see all of your faults in them. It's as if there is a gigantic magnifying glass, constantly revealing their weaknesses, which also happen to be the same weaknesses that you struggle with on a daily basis.

This, of course, creates the perfect breeding ground for fighting, resentment, and hurt. So, as mothers, we have to recognize the situation and take control of it. For example, when my daughter Allyson parked in a "Parking zone" that was a "No parking zone" during certain hours, which she would've know if she'd taken time to read the sign, and received a hefty parking ticket for her negligence, I wanted to throttle her. I knew she didn't have the money to pay for the ticket, and I knew we couldn't tell her dad because that kind of stuff takes his stress level into the danger zone, so that meant dear old Mom would be forking over $75.

I was ticked!

Just as I was about to unleash an irresponsibility lecture upon her, I remembered that I had not one but seven parking tickets when I attended Indiana University. I also remembered that I almost wasn't able to walk in the graduation ceremonies because I hadn't paid them or told my parents that I even had ever received them. And, I remembered that when I did finally tell my mom about the seven tickets, she simply wrote a check and said, "Never speak of this."

She let me off the hook without a lengthy lecture, and she didn't tell my dad who probably would've taken away my car for good. I was given grace; therefore, I needed to pay it forward. So, I didn't lecture Ally. Instead, I told her about my numerous IU parking tickets, and we had a good laugh.

I turned the tables on that "Mother's Curse," and instead of letting Ally's irresponsibility send me into a tizzy, I was able to reflect, regroup, and realize that it wasn't worth getting upset over, and that Ally had a lot of other strengths—paying attention to signage just wasn't one of them.

She truly is her mother's daughter.

It's time for you to break that "Mother's Curse," too, and celebrate your children. We need to smash that magnifying glass that emphasizes their flaws and love our kids—flaws and all. Ask the Lord to help you see your children as God sees them. And, while you're at it, ask Him to help you see yourself through His eyes, too.

In other words, give your kids and yourself a break. Don't expect them to be perfect, and don't expect perfection from yourself, either. God loves you and your children, and He doesn't hold your weaknesses against you, keeping track of every time you've failed. Remember, His power is made perfect through our weakness. Now, that's worth celebrating! (Go ahead and have a box of Milk Duds on me!)

Lastly, we may have the "Mother's Curse," but the "Father's blessing" trumps that every time.

KISSES FROM HEAVEN

My grace is sufficient for you,
for my power is made perfect in weakness.

1 Corinthians 12:9 (NIV)

HEART TO HEAVEN

Father, help me to nurture my children's strengths and pray over their weaknesses. Help to show more grace and love when I parent, the same way that You do to me. And, help me to never lose sight of the fact that children are a blessing from You—especially the ones who act just like me. In the mighty name of Your Son, Jesus, Amen.

CHOCOLATE STARS
IN YOUR EYES ...

STRIVING TO BE
THE PERFECT MOM

MY MAMA MARION MEDLOCK

My mama, Marion Medlock, knew how to cook she just didn't like to cook very much. If Dad would've let her, she probably would've stored her sweaters in the oven like Carrie Bradshaw.

It's safe to say, I take after my mom.

But, my mom had a few specialties that nobody could beat! One of her most revered recipes was her World Famous No Bake Cookies. Now, I have sampled other people's No Bakes, and I've tried to make them a few times myself, but nobody has "the touch" that my mom did. Hers were always moist but not too gooey. They were sweet but not too sweet. They were heaven in a cookie, and I would give anything to have one right now.

Since Mom's passing in 2008, several of us in the family have tried to replicate Mamaw's World Famous No Bake Cookies, but not one of us has it mastered yet; however, my niece Autumn Bailey is definitely on the right track. When Autumn made a double batch for Christmas Eve last year, I must've eaten five right in a row. It was almost like Mom was there with us. The torch has been passed to Autumn in our family. Now, I'm passing it to you for your family.

MAMAW 'S NO BAKE COOKIES

2 cups of sugar

1 stick of butter

½ cup milk

3 level tablespoons of Hershey's dry cocoa

1 teaspoon vanilla

1 ½ cup quick-cooking oats

½ cup creamy peanut butter

Put first 4 ingredients in a sauce pan.

In a separate bowl, put ½ cup peanut butter and 1½ cups of quick-cooking oats.

Next, bring mixture in saucepan to a boil and put a candy thermometer in pan. When the temperature reaches a soft boil, remove from the burner and add 1 teaspoon of vanilla, as well as the peanut butter and oats mixture. Mix it all up and drop spoonfuls onto aluminum foil (shiny side up) or wax paper. Makes about 30 heavenly cookies.

Chapter 19

NOBODY'S PERFECT

You know the problem with trying to be perfect? You always end up disappointed in yourself and others. During the seasons of my life when I've been on the "Pollyanna Perfectionist" kick, striving to be that perfect mom, with the perfectly clean house, the perfect figure, the perfect marriage, and the perfect children, I've noticed I'm always perfectly miserable.

I've also noticed when I get in that perfectionist mode, I not only find fault with everything I do, but also I find fault with everything that others do. As you might imagine, I don't have a lot of friends and family who want to hang out with me when I'm sporting my "Pollyanna Perfectionist" hat. You see, when we have on that hat, we expect perfection from everyone around us, even our children, and when they can't achieve total perfection, we unintentionally crush their little spirits. We're setting them up for failure, and that's not fair.

The dictionary defines perfection like this:

"The quality or condition of being perfect.

The act or process of perfecting.

A person or thing considered to be perfect.

An instance of excellence."

Wow. If I am supposed to be "excellent" all the time, I'm in a heap of trouble. There are some days when I might earn that "Blue Ribbon of Excellence" award for being a good mom, but there are a lot of other days when I wouldn't even qualify for an honorable mention. How about you?

That's why I like the Christian definition of perfection a lot better—"loving God with all our heart, mind, soul and strength."

Now that seems a lot more attainable to me. In other words, I don't always have to "get it right," but if my heart is right, and if I'm truly seeking God, I can walk in Christian Perfection all day, every day. And, guess what?

So, can you!

Even if you're the mom who orders her children's birthday cakes from the bakery instead of creating them from scratch, it's OK. (By the way, that'd be me.) Even if you burn at least one batch of chocolate chip cookies every time you bake, it's fine. (Guilty again.) Even if your house is overrun with life-size dust bunnies once in a while, it's OK. Even if your waist is no longer a size 4, it's totally fine. And, even if you occasionally yell at your children and have to apologize later for losing your temper, it's all right. We aren't striving for the world's definition of perfection, so quit putting those demands on yourself and everybody else in your life. Rest in the Lord and meditate on His definition of perfection, which is "loving Him with all of your heart, mind, soul, and strength."

Now, I'm not saying we should just set up camp at "Mount Mediocre" and settle there forever. No, we should strive to be better and more like Jesus every day. But, on the days when we fall plumb off the mountain, we have to be able to forgive ourselves and climb back up.

If you're still having trouble removing that "Pollyanna Perfectionist" hat, ask God to help you accept yourself as human and move on. Listen, we may never win another "Best Mom Blue Ribbon" the rest of our lives, but we can still be winners. Who says nobody's perfect? If we're in love with God, He says we are!

KISSES FROM HEAVEN

To all perfection I see a limit;
but your commands are boundless.

Psalm 119:96 (NIV)

HEART TO HEAVEN

Father, help me to lose my "Pollyanna Perfectionist" hat and stop striving for the world's definition of perfection. Help me to fall more in love with You and become more like You every single day. And, God, help me not to place unrealistic expectations on my children, setting them up for failure. Rather, help me to encourage them to be the best they can be but never pressure them into thinking they have to be perfect. In the mighty name of Your Son, Jesus, Amen.

Chapter 20

YOU ARE CALLED AND EQUIPPED

Not long ago as I stood in the security line at LAX, I couldn't help but notice the family in front of me. The mom obviously had her hands full, traveling with her son who was about 8 years old, as well as an infant daughter in a stroller. Plus, she was lugging around a car seat and two backpacks. As they waited their turn, I noticed the boy kept fidgeting and trying to go beyond the rope barrier. This mama calmly instructed him to stop several times, never losing her calm demeanor. As she struggled to get the baby out of the stroller in preparation to go through the security scanner, the boy pushed past the rope barrier and into the forbidden area, prompting a security guard to come over and harshly reprimand the boy. The mama stepped between her son and the security guard and promised it wouldn't happen again. It became obvious that this young boy had some special needs.

After the security guard encounter, he covered his ears and dropped to the floor in a small ball. Without hesitation, this mama knelt down and spoke gently but firmly to her son, explaining that he would get in very big trouble with the security guard if he crossed the line again. Then she hugged her son and kissed him on the forehead before standing up to once again unstrap her baby from the stroller.

I so wanted to step in and help, and just as I was about to offer my assistance, that mama was motioned forward to go through the security scanner. I think everyone in line breathed a sigh of relief as she made it through security on the very first try.

That amazing mama took care of both of her children, handling the stressful situation with grace, dignity, and love. If they had medals for motherhood, she definitely earned one in just those 15 minutes that I observed her. She exuded love and patience from every pore. It was almost like she had this supernatural peace about her that even a very expressive and agitated security guard couldn't rattle. I'm not sure if she was a Christian, but based on what I observed, I'd say she would have to be a believer.

Later, as I thought about this amazing mother, I realized that God truly does give us whatever we need in order to handle any situation we encounter. The Word tells us that we can do all things through Christ who gives us strength, but do we live like that's true? Do we really have a revelation of that verse? Or, do we just say the verse from memory before retreating under our beds with a box of chocolates, never realizing the power of its words? I challenge you to say, "I can do all things through Christ who strengthens me" out loud several times today and every day, reminding yourself that you are called and equipped to be a great mother. Whether you have a special needs child or you're a single mom; whether you have a child battling a serious illness or you have a teenager who has walked away from God; you can do this! And, you don't have to go it alone. God promises to never leave you nor forsake you, so lean on Him. You've got this, and He's got you.

KISSES FROM HEAVEN

But those who hope in the Lord will renew their strength. They will soar on wings like eagles; they will run and not grow weary, they will walk and not be faint.

Isaiah 40:31 (NIV)

HEART TO HEAVEN

Father, thank You for calling me and equipping me to fulfill my divine destiny in You. And, help me, Lord, to never forget that I can do all things through Christ who strengthens me. I pray, God, that just by living my life and handling every situation with love and grace that I'll be a witness to many, giving me the chance to share my faith. In the mighty name of Jesus, Amen.

Chapter 21

WALK IN YOUR CALLING

Not long ago, I was flipping through TV channels and ran across "LIFE Today" hosted by James and Betty Robison. That day's show featured writer, director, and producer Randall Wallace, best known for penning "Braveheart" and directing "We Were Soldiers" and "Secretariat." Wallace was there to discuss the very popular "Heaven Is for Real" that he also directed. I love that movie so much, so I took time to watch the program that morning. During the course of the interview, James Robison noted that it's obvious Wallace is very selective when choosing projects, as many of them tell wonderful, uplifting stories that have a spiritual application.

"You want people to know the Lord . . . you want people to know Christ and know him personally? Is that right?" James Robison asked.

Wallace thought for a moment and then answered, "I was a seminary student . . . I left the seminary thinking that I wasn't getting the call, so I spoke to my family pastor. He knew I was studying religion in school and he said, 'Do you feel the call to pastor?' I said, 'Honestly, I don't, though I know it is the greatest call anyone can have,' and he said, 'You're wrong. The greatest call you can have is the one God has for you.'"

Wallace went on to say that his call is to tell inspiring stories and to tell the truth as he knows it. He is thankful to be walking in his calling.

I am thankful Wallace is walking in his calling, too, or we might never have seen his inspiring films. I didn't want to forget those powerful words he shared, so I wrote them down and stuck them in my Bible.

I don't want you to forget them, either.

Just because you weren't called to be a pastor doesn't mean you won't impact the world with the love of God in your own way. Maybe you will never preach a sermon about kindness, but you show kindness to that homeless man every day when you pass him on your daily walk. Maybe you'll never write a book about the love of God, but you have your own children write letters of encouragement to soldiers overseas every holiday season.

You don't have to be behind a pulpit to have divine purpose.

Whether you're called to be a CEO, a teacher, or a stay-at-home mom, you are important. Your life means something. As mothers, we have the most important job—raising kids who love the Lord and helping them discover their divine purpose. God called you to fulfill that special role because He trusts you. In fact, God has had a plan for your life from the time you were in your mother's womb. It's so powerful when you realize that you're doing exactly what you were born to do, and the devil knows this truth. That's why he will do everything he can to discourage you and get you to compare yourself with others and their callings, trying to convince you that your calling is not as important.

But it is!

Don't fall for his lies. Instead, thank God for your calling and walk in it with great enthusiasm and courage. Run your race—fueled by God's Word and a piece of chocolate now and again. When you do, you'll enjoy the journey, and every step toward that finish line will be purposeful.

KISSES FROM HEAVEN

Therefore, since we are surrounded by such a great cloud of witnesses, let us throw off everything that hinders and the sin that so easily entangles. And let us run with perseverance the race marked out for us.

Hebrews 12:1 (NIV)

HEART TO HEAVEN

Father, I thank You for creating me for such a time as this. Help me to never forget the importance of my calling, and help me to fulfill my divine destiny. I love You, Lord. In the mighty name of Jesus. Amen.

Chapter 22

IDENTITY CRISIS SOLVED

Before I had children, I was a newspaper reporter for an Indiana daily newspaper, covering important local stories and even interviewing celebrities from time to time. When I went places in our readership area, people I'd never met before "knew me" and spoke to me about past stories I'd written or offered ideas for new pieces I should pursue.

I liked being Michelle Adams, newspaper reporter.

But, after I had our daughters, Abby and Ally, I eventually gave up my crazy life as a newspaper reporter to stay home and be a mommy while trying to build a freelance writing career. Suddenly, my day went from morning news meetings to morning cartoons.

Life had changed, and I hadn't been prepared for it.

About a year after leaving the newspaper, my husband's CPA firm was invited to a Chamber of Commerce event, so of course, I went as Jeff's date. As we mingled that night, chatting it up with the local movers and shakers, it was obvious I was no longer in the "in crowd."

I had transformed from "Michelle Adams, newspaper reporter" to simply Jeff's wife and Abby's and Ally's mother. I had little to contribute to conversation since no one at the party seemed to care that the new and improved Ovaltine actually tasted like yummy chocolate milk. Eventually, I gave up and left the corporate side of the room to find the other mommies. Thankfully, the mommy group was extremely accepting, and we talked about recent toy recalls, formula versus breast feeding and the "Disney on Ice" event that was coming to Indianapolis the following month.

Still, when Jeff and I headed home that night, I felt unimportant and frustrated.

"Something wrong?" Jeff asked, grabbing my hand across the console.

"No, not really," I said. "I guess I realized tonight that I've lost my identity. I just have to figure out who I am again."

Those words hung in the air the rest of the ride home. I felt guilty for even having those thoughts. Here I'd gotten exactly what I wanted, and now I wasn't sure I wanted it.

My mom, our go-to babysitter, had already put the girls to bed by the time we arrived home. I gently kissed Abby on her forehead, careful not to wake her, and then did the same for Ally. As I closed the door behind me, I couldn't help but smile, so thankful for my girls and so grateful to be their mommy. I realized at that moment that I wasn't longing for my old life as a newspaper reporter. I loved my life. What I missed was the title and identity that went along with my newspaper job.

That night was the beginning and end of my identity crisis. I spent some time with the Lord before going to bed, and I re-discovered that my identity was in Christ—period. No matter the season of my life. No matter if I wore the mommy hat or the writer hat on that particular day. If I was surrounded by newsroom full of fellow reporters chasing down stories or a sea of sippy cups and pacifiers—I was still me. And that "me" was fully committed to my Heavenly Father. It didn't matter that the movers and shakers no longer knew my name because the Creator of the universe knew my name and had even recorded it in the Lamb's Book of Life!

So, if you're in the middle of an identity crisis—here's your answer. You are a child of the Most High God. Through job changes, geographic moves, name changes, church divisions, family separations, different seasons of life—through it all—God is never changing, and His love for you is steadfast. As Christians, our identity is in Christ, and that's more than enough.

KISSES FROM HEAVEN

*For we are God's masterpiece. He has created us
anew in Christ Jesus, so we can do
the good things he planned for us long ago.*
Ephesians 2:10 (NLT)

HEART TO HEAVEN

Father, I am so thankful my identity is in You. Help
me to never lose sight of that fact. In the Name of
Jesus. Amen.

Chapter 23

WORMS AND ALL

I grew up watching reruns of "Leave It to Beaver" and "The Brady Bunch," and I thought June Cleaver and Carol Brady had to be the coolest moms in the entire world. Both seemed to have it all together. Their husbands adored them, and their children loved and honored them. June and Carol seemed to handle everything life threw at them with grace and humor, all the while looking like a million bucks. June in her crisp, white apron and Carol with her adorable shag haircut. June could whip up a magnificent dinner every night without breaking a sweat, not to mention the freshly baked chocolate chip cookies she always had awaiting her sons. And Carol managed a household of six children and still found time to volunteer and sing in the church choir. (Of course, to be fair, Carol had Alice the housekeeper to help her . . . boy, I sure could've used Alice when my children were young.) Yep, I decided when I became a mom, I wanted to be a combination of June and Carol . . . but that so didn't happen. I'm afraid I have fallen far short of that goal. I've never even owned an apron, and my dinners typically involve a crockpot. I definitely don't sing in the church choir, but I have volunteered at the girls' school functions many times, sporting big 80s hair—not the shag, sorry Carol. Still, in my mind, my best never seemed to measure up to the ideal mom I had concocted in my imagination.

In fact, there have been days when I looked at my children and wondered if God really knew what He was doing when He entrusted me with such amazing girls. But then I'll think: *He's God. He knew all of my shortcomings and faults even before I became a mother, so He must see potential in me that I don't see.*

Aren't you thankful that God looks at us through eyes of love instead of eyes of judgment and condemnation? On the days when I burn our family dinner, misplace an important sports jersey, lose the signed permission slip, or miss an important event in my children's lives due to work obligations, I am immensely thankful that God is a patient, loving, always-seeing-the-best-in-me kind of God. I bet you are, too.

So, while it's true I haven't achieved June Cleaver or Carol Brady status, I've definitely become a better version of Michelle Adams over the years. And, God has been with me every step of the way, changing me and perfecting me from glory to glory. And, He's doing the same for you! He understands when we miss the mark. He cheers us on when we take a step closer to Him. He loves it when we are quick repenters and embrace His correction. Bottom line, He loves us even more than we love our own children. Think about that for a moment. You love your children so much that you'd give your life for them, and I'd do the same. Well, Jesus already gave His life for us. That's how much He loves us—in spite of our shortcomings and less-than-perfect motherhood moments.

So, the next time you feel overwhelmed, less than worthy and totally clueless—ask God to help you see yourself the way He sees you. He adores you. You're the apple of His eye—worms and all. ☺

KISSES FROM HEAVEN

Not that I have already obtained all this,
or have already been made perfect,
but I press on to take hold of that for which
Christ Jesus took hold of me.
Philippians 3:12 (NIV)

HEART TO HEAVEN

Father, I praise You for seeing the best in me and for perfecting me from glory to glory. Thanks for never giving up on me even when I want to give up on myself. Help me, God, to see myself as You see me, through eyes of unconditional love. I love You, God. In the mighty name of Jesus, Amen.

Chapter 24

ARE YOU A QUIET CUBBIE?

For my daughter Ally's 20th birthday, she asked for only one thing—tickets to see the Cubs play the Dodgers when the Cubbies rolled into Los Angeles—so I gladly obliged. I purchased excellent tickets from a season ticketholder who couldn't go, and we planned for a fun night. Of course, these tickets were right in the heart of die-hard Dodgers fans, and normally that wouldn't be an issue; I'd just blend in and enjoy a great game of baseball. But, you see, I'm a die-hard Cubs fan.

And, I don't just back the Cubs because I'm from the Midwest—my love for the Cubs goes way deeper than that. I love the Chicago Cubs because my daddy loved them. Much of my childhood, I was blessed to go road-trippin' with the Cubbies. Mom, Daddy, and I would pile in our long, white

Caddy and head off to wherever the Cubs were playing that night.

As you can imagine, I really wanted to wear one of my bedazzled Cubs shirts to the game with Ally, but knowing that the Cubs had badly beaten the Dodgers the night before, I was nervous I might be provoking some passionate Dodgers fans who would surely be surrounding us.

So, I took the cowardly Cubs fan way out and wore red—sort of a non-biased team color.

When we arrived in our seats, I was so surprised to see an entire row of Cubs fans right in front of us—all proudly wearing their Cubs jerseys and hats. They cheered and hollered for their beloved Cubbies, despite the heckling from nearby Dodgers die-hards, while I clapped politely. The Cubs ended up losing in extra innings. Still, I enjoyed spending time with my youngest daughter, and my mini plastic Dodgers hat filled with chocolate ice cream; however, I wish I'd worn my Cubs attire.

Later as I reflected on our night at Dodger Stadium, I felt almost guilty that I hadn't represented my team in the midst of the Dodgers fans. Don't get me wrong; I will cheer for the Dodgers when they play any other team BUT the Cubs. But that night, I was a very quiet Cubbies fan, and that's not like me at all.

It made me wonder if that carries over into my spiritual life. Am I a quiet Christian, afraid I might offend those around me who aren't living for God?

Are you?

When your child is asked to a sleepover and you learn they are going to be watching a rated R movie, do you suggest a more kid-friendly movie? Or, do you compromise and say, "It's all right just this once . . . "

As moms, we're faced with situations like this all the time, and I think there's a fine line between being an all-out Christian and being an overly-aggressive Spiritual Sally. I think we have to make decisions that are Bible based and best for our children, but I'll never be someone who works "Praise the Lord!" into every conversation. Still, I hope I am more than just a quiet witness for Jesus without being overly obnoxious about my faith. I pray that I'm a good witness for Jesus—in both words and actions—and that I teach my children to stand up for what they believe.

I pray those same things for you. Let's be bold for our Lord. Let's win others to Jesus by our love. And, let's be unashamed of our walk of faith even though many around us might be on another road. Amen?

Oh, and go Cubs!

KISSES FROM HEAVEN

But in your hearts honor Christ the Lord as holy,
always being prepared to make a defense to
anyone who asks you for a reason for the hope that
is in you; yet do it with gentleness and respect . . .

1 Peter 3:15 (ESV)

HEART TO HEAVEN

Father, help me to be bold about my faith but in a way that's approachable so that others might be drawn to You because of my witness. And, help me, Lord, to show my children how to stand up for their faith without fear. I love You, God. In the mighty name of Jesus, Amen.

SPRINKLES OF HAPPINESS...

FINDING JOY
IN THE JOURNEY

MY COUSIN BROOKE FLEETWOOD AURS

The year that Brooke married her husband, Scott, his parents ended up moving to Florida. Not only did they greatly miss them, but also they greatly missed Scott's mom's fabulous fudge. So, there was only one thing to do in Scott's mind—get the recipe and have Brooke learn how to make his mom's fudge ASAP.

"Yes, I had to pick up the tradition of making the chocolate and peanut butter fudge for Scott," Brooke shared. "Unfortunately, since my mother-in-law wasn't by my side to oversee me the first few times I fixed it, I had to wing it . . . I found myself calling her a lot for cooking advice, though, especially around the holidays."

Apparently, Brooke must've mastered "Sandy's Fudge" because there have been no complaints, only requests for more batches.

SANDY 'S FABULOUS CHOCOLATE & PEANUT BUTTER FUDGE

3 cups of sugar

1 ½ sticks of butter

⅔ cup of sweetened condensed milk

12-ounce bag of semi sweet chocolate chips

1 ½ cups of marshmallow cream

1 teaspoon vanilla

1 cup walnuts (optional)

Put sugar, butter, and condensed milk in pan and bring to a boil. Stir constantly. Keep at a rolling boil for approximately four minutes, and then add chocolate chips, vanilla, and marshmallow cream (and walnuts). Pour into a buttered dish. Refrigerate. Then, enjoy!

Chapter 25

REJOICE IN THE LORD ALWAYS

In Paul's letter to the church at Philippi, he mentions "joy" or "rejoicing" 16 times. What makes that so amazing is this—Paul wasn't writing this letter while eating bon bons in his nice comfy house. He wrote this letter while in prison, and it wasn't just any prison.

Greek scholar and pastor Rick Renner of Renner Ministries studied the historic details of the prison where Paul was being held at the time he wrote to the church at Philippi and shared those findings at one of the church services at Eagle Mountain International Church in Fort Worth, Texas. I'm so thankful I was in that meeting because it forever changed the way I read this passage of Scripture.

It seems that this Roman prison was known as one of the worst prisons in the entire country. It had actually been used as a septic hole for many years and had sort of evolved into a prison for the worst offenders. Prisoners were chained with their arms above their heads and forced to stand waist-deep in human waste. The prisoners had to stand at all times—no matter how weary they grew. And the smell was so horrid, many prisoners died from the toxic fumes alone! Others died from rat bites and infection. Others died from hopelessness.

It was that bad–so awful it sucked the very life right out of many strong men.

The prison was dark all day and all night except for the few moments of limited light when the guard fed the prisoners. There were no windows. No ventilation. No reason for joy.

So, how could Paul write about rejoicing in the Lord in the middle of darkness, depression, and dung? Paul learned that the source of his joy had nothing to do with his environment or his physical state. He found joy in Jesus Christ. That's why Paul was able to write: "Rejoice in the Lord always. I will say it again: Rejoice!"

Paul was living in one of the worst places on all the earth, but his heart was full of joy and Jesus. He knew that Jesus was with him in his suffering, and Paul knew that Jesus would deliver him from that place of despair. Let me ask you this— how is your joy level today? Are you overwhelmed with the worries of today? Are you exhausted and hopeless, wondering if God is actually hearing your prayers? Take a lesson from the Apostle Paul—rejoice no matter what! God is with you! He loves you, and He hasn't forgotten about your situation. Even if you're waist-deep in debt, sickness, marital problems, physical addictions, depression, fear, etc. God is able to deliver you from any of those situations. Even if your child is struggling with an ongoing illness. Even if your grown children are away from the Lord. Even if you've been told you can't have any more children yet you long for more. Nothing is impossible with God (Luke 1:37). So, rejoice! Praise Him! Shout the victory even before you see it!

We used to sing a little chorus at Camp Wildwood in Clay City, Indiana, that simply said: "Praise Him. Praise Him. Praise Him in the morning. Praise Him in the noontime. Praise Him. Praise Him. Praise Him when the sun goes down." That pretty much covers every waking moment, doesn't it? So that's your assignment—praise God all day long! Maybe you can teach your children that little chorus, and you can sing it together every morning before breakfast or on the way to school. Let your family see you praising the Lord and get them involved every chance you get. Or as the Apostle Paul encouraged: "Rejoice in the Lord always—again I say, rejoice!"

KISSES FROM HEAVEN

This is the day which the Lord has made;
let us rejoice and be glad in it.

Psalm 118:24 (NASB)

HEART TO HEAVEN

Father, help me to never lose sight of who You are or let my circumstances determine my joy level. I love You, God, and I am so thankful for another day to rejoice in You! In the mighty name of Jesus, Amen.

Chapter 26

BLONDE FAITH

I am very proud of my daughters, Abby and Ally. Both are beautiful, bright, amazing young women, and I am honored to be their mama. Of course, like the rest of us, they occasionally have a not-so-bright moment that forever becomes part of "the Adams Family Funny Stories File" that we often open and share—all in teasing, of course. One of those moments happened last year when the girls and I had a mom-daughter outing in Hollywood.

It had been a long week of moving Ally into her new apartment, and we were beat. So we decided to go out to dinner, away from the moving boxes and clutter. After finishing our Death by Chocolate dessert, we headed back to the parking garage, ready to call it a night. Abby pushed the button as we awaited on the elevator when all of sudden Ally let out a dramatic sigh of frustration.

"Oh wait, we can't use these elevators," Ally said, motioning to a sign near the elevator.

Too tired to challenge her, both Abby and I followed her around the corner to yet another set of elevators.

"Oh, my gosh," Ally said, visibly upset. "We can't use these elevators either! They're also reserved for firefighters."

Abby looked at me. I looked at Abby. We both looked at the sign, and then we glared at Ally to see if she was being serious.

She was.

True, Ally is my blonde child, but certainly not "a dumb blonde," which made this incident even more hilarious.

"Ally, the sign doesn't say the elevators are reserved for firefighters," Abby explained through giggles. "It says not to use the elevators in case of a fire!"

With that, Ally took a longer look at the sign featuring a little red flame, actually read it instead of skimming it this time, and said, "Oh. Good to know."

The lesson here? You have to take time to read signs, maps, syllabi, directions, recipes, and so on, instead of just assuming you know what they say, or you might go through life climbing many flights of stairs when you could be taking the elevator.

Ally's blonde moment got me thinking about how often we do this with the most important information: the Word of

God. I wonder how many Christians just assume they know what the Bible says instead of actually taking time to read the Scriptures, thus making wrong assumptions and going the wrong direction based on misinformation. How often have I neglected the Bible simply because I think I "know" what it says when I really just need to slow down, open the Word, and meditate on those precious promises? How many times have you done the same?

As moms—whether our children are toddlers or college age—we need all the help we can get, and that help is found in the Word of God. We can't just assume we know what the bible says and simply skim it, hitting "the highlights." That kind of approach leads to pulling out partial truths and jumping to incorrect conclusions, like my sweet Ally with the elevator. Trust me, the consequences will be much worse than climbing several flights of stairs when you could've been riding the elevator. We've been entrusted with precious children to guide and mentor, and we certainly need the wisdom found in the pages of the Word of God to walk in such an important calling. So, make time for God's Word today and every day. Its promises are as sweet as that Death by Chocolate dessert—yum!

KISSES FROM HEAVEN

*All Scripture is breathed out by God and
profitable for teaching, for reproof, for correction,
and for training in righteousness,
that the man of God may be competent,
equipped for every good work.*

2 Timothy 3:16-17 (NKJV)

HEART TO HEAVEN

Father, help me to fall in love with Your Word so that
I'll crave it as much as I crave chocolate. And, Father,
help me to find time to really study Your promises to
me. In the mighty name of Jesus, Amen.

Chapter 27

SLOW DOWN

I zipped past my father carrying an armload of dirty laundry. A few seconds later, I zipped past him again, headed the other direction, with a basket full of clean laundry. A few minutes later, I was rummaging through my desk drawer in search of scissors so I could wrap Allyson's birthday presents, all the while on hold with the local bakery.

"Yes, I want a pink and purple princess cake," I said. "It should say, 'Happy birthday, Allyson . . . that's Allyson with two 'ls' and a 'y.'"

As soon as I finished the call, I glanced up and met Dad's disapproving look.

"You are too busy, honey," he said, sitting in the La-Z-Boy in my living room, watching *The Price Is Right*. "You need to slow down and enjoy life a little more."

He was right.

At that moment, I realized I had been totally ignoring my precious Dad in order to accomplish all of the tasks on my to-do list that morning. All Dad wanted me to do was sit down and spend some quality time with him and Bob Barker. So, I did. I knew the present-wrapping could wait; there would always be a heap of laundry to do; and I could return calls later.

I grabbed my favorite, fuzzy, leopard-print blanket, curled up on the couch, and watched *The Price Is Right* alongside my dad, bidding on items as if I were among the people in Contestant's Row. We laughed and talked and cheered on our favorite contestant in the Showcase Showdown before retreating to the kitchen for a mid-morning snack—chocolate no-bake cookies and coffee. I'm so glad I didn't miss out on that special time with my dad because of an overly-ambitious to-do list.

Daddy passed away a few months later (May 8, 2004), and I'd give anything to spend another morning like that with him, but his words of wisdom remain with me even today.

When I am writing non-stop trying to meet a book deadline or attempting to clean the entire house or organizing my children's closets or trying to do all of those tasks at once (Yes, I believe in multi-tasking!)—I'll hear Dad's words: "You are too busy, honey . . . you need to slow down and enjoy life a little more."

And, so I have been.

The to-do lists will always be, but special times with loved ones can slip by too quickly. The older I get, the more I understand how wise my dad's words were. Slowing down isn't a bad thing—it's a good thing. Remember the old expression: take time to smell the roses? That expression has been around for so long because it holds such truth. God never intended for us to rush through life. We need to enjoy the journey. Celebrate every day—not just the milestones—in our children's lives. We need to stop wishing our lives away, looking toward the next big event or season. Live in the now.

So, watch a game show with your elderly parents. Play a board game with your kiddos. Take a long romantic walk with your spouse. Take time today and every day to simply enjoy life—and maybe a chocolate no-bake cookie, too.

KISSES FROM HEAVEN

How do you know what your life will be like tomorrow? Your life is like the morning fog— it's here a little while, then it's gone.

James 4:14 (NLT)

HEART TO HEAVEN

Father, I know that I allow myself to become too busy and often miss out on special times with loved ones. And, I realize that I become so "to-do list" driven that I sometimes fail to appreciate the beauty around me. So I am asking that You help me prioritize better and slow down enough to enjoy life more. Thank You for loving me and giving me such a wonderful life to enjoy. In the mighty name of Your Son, Jesus, Amen.

Chapter 28

THEY WILL CALL YOU BLESSED . . .

As I was sitting down to write this particular devotion based on Proverbs 31:28 ("Her children arise and call her blessed") my phone bleeped.

It was a text message from my youngest daughter, Allyson, who is finishing up her degree in product development at the Fashion Institute of Design & Merchandising in Los Angeles, 2,200 miles from home.

Glancing at it, I noticed how long the text was, which is not characteristic of Ally's texts. Her texts usually consist of a lot of emojis and no more than two lines. I hoped everything was all right.

It was.

She wrote: "Btw, I never really REALLY realized how blessed I am to have you and dad. I knew I was grateful to have you two but we talked about the average debt for kids coming out of college and how most can't pay for any of it and start their lives paying back school loans. Like the fact you pay for my college is the most amazing thing ever. And then on top of that, my rent, food, bills etc . . . I am so grateful to have you and daddy (and Nana). It's unbelievable how good you guys are to Abby and I. I was just sitting in class while everyone was talking about their debt they already have; how they can't afford anything; and have to work 4 jobs; and I felt horrible for them. I wanted to cry for how amazing you guys are. I just never realized the extent of how blessed I was. So thank you so so so so soooooo much. I need to thank daddy too. Love you!"

Her text brought tears to my eyes. It was actually happening—my children were finally rising up to call me blessed! Let me tell you, there were some parenting days during their teen years when I didn't think we'd ever get to this point—days when "I hate you! You're the worst mom in the entire world!" comments pierced my heart. Of course, I knew my girls didn't mean those hurtful words, but those are still tough to take when you're already questioning your ability to parent.

I think every mother goes through those times when we wonder if we're really capable of raising the children we've been given. On those difficult days, we have to stand on the

Word of God and all of its promises, and we have to know in our knower that God has called us and equipped us to be amazing mothers.

So, press on, my fellow mamas! Your rewards will be great! Now that my girls are 20 and 21, I can testify that it only gets better. They are no longer just my daughters but also my best friends and spiritual sisters. We have long conversations about career paths and love and God and how many calories are in one chocolate donut, and I am constantly amazed by their spiritual maturity, hilarious personalities, and overall awesomeness.

Abby, my oldest, sent me this text a few weeks ago after we'd had one of those deeply spiritual phone conversations the night before:

"I love you, mom & I'm sure you know this already but I really needed to hear everything you said tonight and I'm so thankful that I have such a wonderful, spiritually sound & strong mother like you! You really are my best friend and I look up to you in so many ways. I hope and pray that one day I will be half the woman & mom that you are. I love you so much & I can't wait to be home on Wednesday. Ab"

Talk about seeing Proverbs 31:28 come to life! I am one blessed mama, and so are you.

KISSES FROM HEAVEN

Behold, children are a heritage from the Lord,
the fruit of the womb a reward.

Psalm 127:3 (ESV)

HEART TO HEAVEN

Father, thank You for my children. Help me to be reminded of Your promises on the days when being a mom is really hard. I love You, Lord, and I'm so thankful You called me to be a mother. In the mighty name of Jesus. Amen.

Chapter 29

WAH WAH . . .

If you've ever watched "Saturday Night Live," you've no doubt seen a "Debbie Downer" skit. They are absolutely hilarious! As her name denotes, Debbie Downer (played by Rachel Dratch), was a character who always brought negativity and bad news to a social gathering, thus bringing down the mood of everyone in the room.

For example, in one SNL skit, Debbie Downer is at the happiest place in the world—Disneyland—with her family, enjoying Mickey's Breakfast Jamboree, and the conversation begins.

"Good morning! Welcome to Mickey's Breakfast Jamboree! My name is Billiam, and I'll be serving you today. You guys here on a special occasion?"

"Well, we're here on that new Magical Gatherings family

package," one brother says. "We've got the McKusick clan down from Ohio—right, guys? Say hi!"

"Hi!"

"Well, great," the waiter says. "Let me tell you Mickey's specials today. We've got steak and eggs, served with some home fries and Mickey waffles."

"Whoo hoo!" another brother says. "I love me some steak and eggs!"

"Ever since they found Mad Cow Disease in the U.S., I'm not taking any chances. It can live in your body for years, before it ravages your brain."

Then the camera zooms in on Debbie's face, and the "wah wah" sound effect goes off.

Debbie even had her own theme song: "You're enjoying your day, everything's going your way, when along comes Debbie Downer. Always there to tell you 'bout a new disease, a car accident, or killer bees. You beg her to spare you, 'Debbie, please!' but you can't stop Debbie Downer!"

If we're being honest, there's a Debbie Downer in every family. (Hopefully it's not you!) And, it just takes one Debbie Downer or one Ned Negative to ruin a bunch of Polly and Paul Positives. Before you know it, everybody is in a bad mood.

Both of my girls have always been pretty happy, but growing up, Abby had a tendency to worry. Her worst bouts of worry usually happened on our 45-minute drive to gymnastics. I could always tell when the transformation from Polly Positive to Debbie Downer was about to happen, and I didn't need a "wah wah" sound effect to let me know. Ab would begin sighing.

Well, worry is rooted in fear, and I know from the Word of God that perfect love casts out all fear. So when Abby's sighing began, so did the loving. I would tell Abby everything I loved about her—from her chubby little feet to her big green eyes. She would always act like she didn't like all the positive attention, but deep down, I knew she did because the sighing decreased.

Then, I would shift our attention to God, and we would name all of the reasons that we loved Him. And, then I'd pop in a praise and worship CD, and we'd begin singing at the tops of our lungs. Abby's favorite CD was Janny Grein's "Covenant Woman."

She and Ally would belt out the lyrics: "I've got my feet planted deep in the good, good Word. Standing on the promises that I've heard. Signed, sealed, delivered by the Blood of Lamb. I'm not moved by what I feel. Oh, I'm only moved by the Word that's real. Word came to life. Came to me. I'm a Covenant Woman . . . "

Guess what? You can't be a Covenant Woman and a Debbie Downer at the same time, so Abby's sighing would cease and the joy would return. Worked every time.

So, if you have a Debbie Downer or a Ned Negative living in your house, it's time for a love-fest and a praise-a-thon! As mamas, we set the tone in the home, and that goes for the SUV, too. So, take charge and put the joy back into your family. (Did I mention a little chocolate ice cream is always good, too?)

KISSES FROM HEAVEN

Worry weighs a person down;
an encouraging word cheers a person up.

Proverbs 12:25 (NLT)

HEART TO HEAVEN

Father, please fill my family up with more love and more joy. You are an awesome God! In the mighty name of Jesus. Amen.

CHOCOLATE MELTDOWNS...

LEARNING TO TRUST GOD WHEN BEING A MOM IS DIFFICULT

MY AUNT TAMMY REUTER

Living in a small town, it doesn't take long for word to get around about most anything—especially something involving chocolate. Maybe that's why my Aunt Tammy's mother-in-law, Jeanie, is famous in Lawrence County, Indiana. Her amazing chocolate pie has put her in celebrity status in these parts.

Jeanie Reuter's chocolate pies became a thing of wonder at her church socials. They were also first to go, so if you wanted a piece, you'd have to be quick to the dessert table. One of the firefighters in town who also went to the same church was especially fond of Jeanie's chocolate pies. He always said, "Nobody can make a chocolate pie like her."

He passed away in 2014, and at the family's dinner at the church, Jeanie made a special chocolate pie in his honor. His wife later wrote a thank-you note to Jeanie, saying: "Thank you for making Dennis his last chocolate pie. I had to eat a piece for him."

JEANIE'S CHOCOLATE PIE

2 eggs

1 ¼ cup sugar

⅓ cup cocoa

5 tablespoons cornstarch

1 ¾ cups milk

¾ cup evaporated milk

1 teaspoon vanilla

1 teaspoon butter

1 pre-made 8-inch pie crust, baked as instructed on package.

Beat eggs' yolks; add sugar, cocoa, cornstarch, evaporated milk, and milk. Cook until thick. Stir in vanilla and butter. Put in baked pie crust. Top with meringue* or whipped cream.

*You are on your own for the meringue.

Chapter 30

GOD IS AT WORK

Did you know that God is often working the most when we see it the least?

As I reflect back over my life, that's often been the case. The times when it looked the worst, the times when it seemed like God had gone on vacation—those were the times when God was working behind the scenes on my behalf. What we discover is that our timing is not always God's timing. Actually, our timing is almost never God's timing. We are an instant, give-it-to-me-now society. We want to pray and have God answer us by noon. Wouldn't that be great?

Well, God doesn't usually work like that.

Take it from Noah.

He followed God's leading and built an ark—even though it had never rained before. Then, he followed God's instruction and gathered two of every animal and began filling the big boat. Finally, he and his family boarded the boat and the rain started.

You know the story. You've probably read it to your children many times. It rained 40 days and 40 nights, and Noah and his family were the only ones spared. However, the boat ride was much longer than 40 days. It went on for months and months and months! Think about this for a moment. Noah and his family are on an ark with a bunch of smelly animals for months on end, and there is no land in sight. Can't you just hear his wife saying, "Yeah, great plan, Noah. Where's the land? Did God tell you how long we'd have to float around with a bunch of stinking creatures?" (And, I'm pretty sure they didn't even have any chocolate on board to get them through the really tough days!)

Every day, Noah would look out of the ark's windows, and all he would see was water on every side. So, Noah sent out a bird, hoping to get proof that land had surfaced somewhere, but the first bird came back empty-beaked. It looked like God had forgotten them. It looked like they were doomed to ride around on a big boat forever. But, God was at work through the wind, receding the water every single day– even on the days when Noah looked at the water all around and wondered if God even cared. In time, they hit dry land, and Noah and his family walked off the ark into a new life, a new beginning. Truly, "the wind" had been at work and the promise was fulfilled!

So, here's my question to you today—are you in the middle of a very long ark ride? Have you wondered if God is even paying attention to what's going on in your life? Have you been praying that your son would turn back to God and yet it appears he is in full-blown rebellion right now? Or, have you been praying that God would cause your children to stop fighting and start acting like loving siblings only to referee so many fights between them that you feel like you should be wearing a black and white shirt? Like Noah, you know you've been obedient to follow God's leading, and yet you only see water on all sides. Don't be discouraged. Instead, rejoice! Land is in sight! God hasn't forgotten about you! He is at work behind the scenes! Be happy today—even if you can't see anything changing. That just means God is really doing some stuff!

KISSES FROM HEAVEN

I am trusting you, O LORD, saying,
"You are my God!" My future is in your hands.

Psalm 31:14-15 (NLT)

HEART TO HEAVEN

Father, I don't understand why I am on this long ark ride right now, but I trust that You're working behind the scenes on my behalf. And in faith, I praise You for working in my life even though I can't see any positive changes with my natural eyes. I am excited about my future, and I know that "the wind" is at work in my life this very minute. In the mighty name of Jesus your Son, Amen.

Chapter 31

WEATHERING THE STORMS OF LIFE

It never failed. With the first boom of thunder, Abby and Allyson were both crawling into bed with us. (Usually, they were crawling into bed, asking Daddy to put on cartoons and begging Mommy to make them hot chocolate, as was our "scary storm routine.") As little girls, they were very afraid of storms. Of course, in their defense, we had some Texas-sized thunderstorms that made me cringe just a little when we lived in Fort Worth. My mama used to call those kind of storms "Toad stranglers."

I had empathy for my daughters because I was also deathly afraid of storms when I was a little girl. I can remember pulling my Holly Hobby sleeping bag over my head and praying, "God, please make the storm go away!"

Today, I find myself praying that same prayer when the storms of life get too scary. When my daughter, Allyson, battled anorexia her senior year of high school, I prayed for God to stop that storm. Though we had her in counseling with a doctor who specialized in athletes battling eating disorders, she didn't seem to be getting any better. She went from a 122-pound power tumbler on the varsity cheer team to an 89-pound skeleton of a girl who wasn't strong enough to even throw a single back handspring. Ally was definitely the talk of our small town, and many of those words were quite hurtful to both Ally and our entire family. Each time, it was like another lightning bolt, another thunder boom. I just wanted her to be better and all of the whispering to end. I wanted Ally to realize that she was a precious child of God and that God had a good plan for her life, according to Jeremiah 29:11. But no matter how much I wanted it, I couldn't make it happen. I couldn't make her eat. I couldn't make her well.

Just as we were making plans to withdraw her at midterm of her senior year and send her to a facility called Remuda Ranch for intensive treatment, the black clouds rolled away enough that we could see a glimmer of sunlight. Ally started getting better, remarkably better. God had intervened! Our prayers had been answered! The storm had ended!

I'll never forget Ally's last appointment with her doctor that spring. He said, "I wish I could bottle whatever it is that made Ally have such a turnaround."

I just smiled and said, "Well, you can't bottle it but you can access it—it's God. He is the reason she is still with us and totally healed."

"We call it remission," he said.

"We call it healed," I answered, and thanked him for all he had done.

Did that storm drag on longer than we would have liked? Absolutely.

Would I rather have had that storm blow past us entirely? Of course!

But in the midst of life's scariest storms—when our children's health is at stake, when there's no money for food, when your spouse says he isn't in love with you anymore— God is there. He promises to never leave us, nor forsake us. True, He doesn't always calm the storms in the way that we want or as quickly as we'd like, but He always comes through. All we have to do is have faith. So, come on out from under the covers and call on the One who can calm the storms in your life and in the lives of your children. Let Him speak peace into your life today!

KISSES FROM HEAVEN

The disciples woke him up, shouting,
"Master, Master, we're going to drown!"
So Jesus rebuked the wind and the raging waves.
The storm stopped and all was calm!

Luke 8:24 (NLT)

HEART TO HEAVEN

Lord, thank You for settling the storms in my life and bringing peace to all situations. In the mighty name of Jesus, Amen.

Chapter 32

DOGGONE FAITH

Have you ever heard the theory that people end up owning the dog breed that they most resemble? Well, I'd have to say that is true when it comes to me.

I am the proud "mama" of a miniature long-haired dachshund named Mollie Mae. She has very short legs and a very distinctive nose. Yeah, I definitely share those same physical characteristics. (You're checking out your dog right now, aren't you?) And, unfortunately, Mollie also loves chocolate like her mama, and chocolate is very bad for dogs. I have to hide my stash high enough so Mollie Mae can't get to it. Yeah, my dachshund and I are a lot alike.

But in the spiritual realm, we all need to resemble English bulldogs. Bible teacher Kate McVeigh once shared that Christians need to have bulldog faith. She said, "A bulldog only knows one thing. That bone is his, and he's taking it." And, that bulldog won't let loose of that bone—no matter what.

Did you know that the English bulldog's jaw muscles are as strong as any athlete's muscles, and when it latches onto something, it really latches on? In fact, PedigreeDatabase .com states that the bite force of an English bulldog can exceed 305 pounds of pressure.

Well, guess what? That's how we have to be when it comes to our faith, especially as faith-filled mamas. It's not just about us and our faith; it's about our children and their faith, too. And, it's up to us to make sure our children grow up knowing the Lord, loving Him, and serving Him.

Of course, I realize that doesn't always happen, even when a child is raised in a Christian home but we have this promise: "Train up a child in the way he should go, and when he is old he will not depart from it" (Proverbs 22:6). That's good news!

So, even if you're reading this right now and feeling brokenhearted because your teenage son or adult daughter is away from God, don't lose faith! Stand on Proverbs 22:6 and begin to praise the Lord that your child is a mighty man or woman of God—even if you can't see it yet with your natural eyes. Get that bulldog faith on! Lock your jaws on that promise and don't turn loose of it! It's yours!

Here's some more encouragement for you. Mark 11:23-24 says: "I tell you the truth, if anyone says to this mountain, 'Go, throw yourself into the sea,' and does not doubt in his heart but believes that what he says will happen, it will be done for him. Therefore I tell you, whatever you ask for in prayer, believe that you have received it, and it will be yours."

In other words, you have to believe that your child is free from drugs, even if that hasn't happened yet. You have to believe that your child will return to God, even if she seems to have hardened her heart toward you and anything to do with God. You have to believe that your son who is deployed overseas is safe and protected, even if you don't hear from him for several weeks in a row. Get a lockjaw of faith on whatever it is you're trusting God to do in your life or in the lives of your children, and don't turn loose until the desired result comes! Growl in the face of adversity and develop that bulldog faith. Our kids are counting on us.

KISSES FROM HEAVEN

Now faith is the substance of things hoped for,
the evidence of things not seen.

Hebrews 11:1 (NKJV)

HEART TO HEAVEN

Father, I want to have the kind of bulldog faith that it takes to believe for the miracle breakthroughs I need in my family without giving up or letting go. Help me, Lord, to hang on and stand on Your Word. I give my children to You, Lord, and I praise You that they are mighty in faith! I love You, and I trust You. In the mighty name of Jesus. Amen.

Chapter 33

HOPEFULLY DEVOTED

While spending time with my daughter Allyson at her apartment in Los Angeles last year, we decided to watch a movie, eat chocolate cupcakes from Sprinkles, and enjoy a "girls' night in." Only one problem—we couldn't find a movie that we wanted to rent.

Just as I was about to give up on movie night, Ally grabbed the remote and began scrolling through all of the movies she had recorded from TV until she finally landed on *Grease.*

"No way!" I said, smiling as if I'd just been cast opposite John Travolta.

Probably like many of you, I grew up watching *Grease,* starring John Travolta and Olivia Newton-John.

My favorite scene? I love it when Olivia Newton-John, looking innocent and gorgeous in her simple nightgown, walks around the baby pool in the backyard singing, "Hopelessly Devoted to You." (You're singing along right now, aren't you?)

Hopelessly devoted.

Dictionary.com defines devotion as: "a commitment to some purpose; or a religious zeal; a willingness to serve God."

Devotion is a very noble character trait, something mamas know a lot about. You can see glimpses of devotion in everyday life. And, if you spend much time reading God's Word, you'll definitely encounter examples of devotion—especially in the story of the Cross.

Jesus was devoted to the Father—so much so—that he was willing to die to fulfill God's salvation plan so that we could spend eternity with Him. And, though some of Jesus's followers disassociated themselves from Jesus for fear of being crucified, too, the women didn't disown Him.

The women. The mamas. They stayed.

It tells us in John 19:25 that Mary, the mother of Jesus; Jesus's aunt; Mary the wife of Clopas; and Mary Magdalene stayed at the foot of the cross, even though they were implicating themselves just by being there.

They were devoted to Him. They loved Him more than they loved themselves. They were willing to stay with Him until the very end. Even though I've read that passage of Scripture many times, the last time I read it, I was taken aback by the devotion of these women. I wondered, "Would I have stayed at the foot of the cross, knowing I might be punished severely for showing my love and support of Jesus? Would I have been so devoted?"

Would you?

Are you devoted to Jesus? Do you love Him more than you love yourself? Here's a tough one. Do you love Him more than you love your children? And, do you really trust Him with your children? I find myself struggling with this one, now that my girls are older, making those big life decisions. For example, my oldest daughter Abby is majoring in early childhood education, and just the other day she said, "Mom, I feel like I am supposed to do a missions trip and work with children overseas . . . what do you think?"

My flesh wanted to say, "Uhh . . . no. Have you been watching the news? Terrorism is so prevalent right now, and they're targeting Americans. Why not just teach VBS this summer at our church?"

But, as a mom who is devoted to God and trusts Him with my children, I simply said, "Honestly, Ab, the idea of you going overseas right now really scares me, but if you've heard from God and feel very strongly that you're supposed to do a missions trip, let's research some possibilities."

Bottom line, we're either devoted to God, or we're not. We either trust Him, or we don't. So, if like me, you're unsure of your level of devotion and struggling with fully trusting Him with your children, then it's time to sit at the foot of the cross, just basking in His presence.

When we do that, unlike Olivia Newton-John, we won't be "hopelessly devoted" to Jesus; rather, we'll become "*Hopefully* Devoted."

KISSES FROM HEAVEN
Near the cross of Jesus stood his mother,
his mother's sister, Mary the wife of Clopas,
and Mary Magdalene.
John 19:25 (NIV)

HEART TO HEAVEN
Father, I fully devote myself to You. Help me, Lord, to fully trust You with my children—at every stage of their lives. In the mighty name of Jesus. Amen.

Chapter 34

LIFE IS LIKE A BOX OF CHOCOLATES . . .

In the opening scenes of the movie *Forrest Gump*, Tom Hanks, who plays Forrest, is sitting on a bench with a box of chocolates on his lap. Soon, a woman sits down on the other side of the bench.

"Hello. My name's Forrest. Forrest Gump . . . You want a chocolate?"

The woman never even looks up from her magazine.

"My mama always said, 'Life was like a box of chocolates,'" he continues, while chewing a piece of chocolate. "You never know what you're gonna get."

There's a lot of truth in that bit of dialogue.

I also think that parenting is a lot like a box of chocolates. Some days you get your favorite caramel nut, milk chocolate covered piece, and other days you bite into the nasty orange cream-filled piece! Not every day can be a caramel nut, milk chocolate kind of day. Nah, you have to have a few orange cream-filled days to make you appreciate the really good ones.

I remember one of those "orange cream-filled days" very well. I dropped off Ally, who was in middle school at the time, at our cousin's shop to get her hair trimmed and highlighted while I went on to my business luncheon. At the conclusion of my meeting, I noticed that my husband had called several times. That wasn't like him.

"Everything OK, babe?" I asked.

"Uhh . . . what was Ally supposed to get done to her hair?"

"Trimmed and highlighted, why?" I asked, nervously.

"Well, something must've gone drastically wrong then."

I sped home, and when I walked into Ally's room, I saw it. Her once long hair was cut in short layers on top, sticking up sort of like a Punk Rock rooster. The back remained long but thinned out somehow, reminiscent of a grown out mullet. I just couldn't figure out what had happened.

"Did your hair break off in the foils?" I asked.

"No," Ally said. "I like it."

I left her room and called our cousin, who is an amazing stylist, to find out what had happened. I knew there had to be an explanation for this horrendous hairdo.

Turns out, my little Barbie doll daughter decided she didn't want to look like a Barbie anymore and printed a picture off the Internet, took it to our cousin without me knowing, and said, "This is how I want my hair." He, of course, thought I had approved.

Ally was happy; I was not.

I had to ground Ally for lying and being sneaky, although I felt like her horrible hair was punishment enough. Later that night, as I was telling the girls goodnight, I asked Ally: "Honey, why did you want to do that to your hair?"

She looked up at me with tear-filled eyes and said, "I just wanted to stand out, Mom. I just wanted to feel special like I did in Texas."

I hadn't even considered that, but all at once I understood. We had moved the girls from Texas back to Indiana during their middle school years, making them leave their cheer squads, their best friends, and their school—a school where they were popular and knew everyone. Ally wasn't adjusting as well as I'd hoped.

I hugged her and told her I understood. We prayed together, and I asked God to heal her heart and send her a best friend.

Not long after, a pretty little girl with big brown eyes and the same crazy haircut showed up at our house. Her name was Jill, Ally's new best friend. God had answered our prayers.

He'll answer your prayers, too.

So, if you're having a run of orange cream-filled pieces, hang on! A caramel nut, milk chocolate piece is on its way.

KISSES FROM HEAVEN

Dear brothers and sisters, when troubles of any kind come your way, consider it an opportunity for great joy. For you know that when your faith is tested, your endurance has a chance to grow.

James 1:2-3 (NLT)

HEART TO HEAVEN

Father, thank You for the good days and the not-so-good days when we can see Your faithfulness. In the mighty name of Jesus. Amen.

TRUFFLES OF TEACHABLE MOMENTS...

LEARNING LESSONS FROM OUR CHILDREN

MY SISTER MARTIE MEDLOCK SPAULDING

A trained interior designer and a gifted cook, my sister is just like Martha Stewart. And . . . I'm more like Jimmy Stewart. But, thankfully Martie hosts all of our family get-togethers, and when we have pitch-ins, I'm typically assigned rolls and soda. (You can't really mess up on those!)

One of our family's favorite desserts is my Grandma Medlock's French Silk Pie, and Martie has mastered it. While all chocolate pies are pretty much a homerun in my book, this particular French Silk Chocolate Pie is the creamiest, silkiest, melt-in-your-mouth dessert you'll ever eat. It's a lighter, less strong chocolate pie, which makes it perfect for even those who aren't big fans of chocolate. (We'll pray for them, haha.)

GRANDMA MEDLOCK'S
FRENCH SILK CHOCOLATE PIE

½ cup butter

¾ cup sugar

3 ounces of unsweetened chocolate, cut into pieces

1 teaspoon vanilla

2 eggs

Topping:

½ cup sweetened whipped cream

Chocolate curls, if desired

Bake an 8-inch pie shell until golden brown, and set aside to cool. In a small bowl, beat butter and sugar on medium speed until the mixture is fluffy. In a saucepan, melt chocolate over low heat. After the melted chocolate cools, add the vanilla. Gradually beat in cooled chocolate and vanilla mixture until well blended. Add eggs one at a time, and beat on medium speed for 5 minutes after adding each egg. (Scrape the sides of the bowl occasionally.) Pour into cooled baked shell. Refrigerate at least 2 hours before serving. Garnish with whipped cream and chocolate curls. Cover and refrigerate any remaining pie.

Chapter 35

DALMATIAN COWS AND OTHER BLESSINGS

It had been one of those days. One of the dogs had thrown up on the living room carpet. My editor had passed me over for a major project that had originally been promised to me. The air conditioning in our Ford Explorer had gone out. And, I'd spilled orange pop all over the front of my white blouse. I just wanted to go home, throw on my nightgown, relax in the recliner, and have a Snickers and a Diet Coke.

Ever been there?

My mind replayed the stressful day as the girls and I headed home. I was caught up in "the feeling sorry for myself mode" when my thoughts were interrupted by a high-pitched squeal coming from the backseat.

"Look, Mommy!" Allyson shrieked with glee.

"What, honey? Look at what?" I asked, glancing out my side window to see a field full of Holstein cows.

"Look, Mommy! A Dalmatian cow!" she said.

It took a moment for my mind to process what she'd said—a Dalmatian cow.

"Oh, you mean those black and white cows in that field?" I asked, trying not to laugh.

"Uh huh," she said, excitedly.

Kids are funny, I thought. *They see things in such a different light.*

As I loaded the dishwasher that evening, still feeling a little depressed about my terrible day, my mind kept drifting back to Allyson's Dalmatian cows. The more I thought about it, the more I realized there was much to be learned from her funny comment.

I had looked out the SUV window, and all I had observed was a field full of Holstein cows—a sight I'd seen hundreds of times in my life—so I didn't give it a second thought. And, I certainly didn't appreciate it.

But, Allyson did.

She looked at the same field and rejoiced over Dalmatian cows.

I realized that it had been a long time since I'd been truly thankful for anything that God had done for me. Sure, I praised Him a little every day during my quiet time, but I certainly wasn't looking for new reasons to sing His praises. In other words, I wasn't searching for fields of Dalmatian cows to appreciate Him.

I determined in my heart to make a change that very moment.

"Help me, Lord, to see things as Allyson does," I prayed. "Help me to be quick to notice the good things You've done and to keep a grateful heart at all times."

Then, I began praising God for the many blessings in my life. As I praised Him for my godly husband, my two precious children, my wonderful parents and in-laws, my sister and brother and their families, our good health, our home— the fog began to lift.

Ally saw those Dalmatian cows over 15 years ago, and I still think about them quite often. So, am I singing God's praises all of the time? Well, let's just say I've gotten better at it over the years. Now, when I am having one of those days when the dog has thrown up on the carpet or an editor has rejected one of my articles, I get "my praise on" (and yes, I still have a Snickers and a Diet Coke), and soon the fog lifts.

If you've been a little "foggy" lately, just raise your hands to the Father and get your praise on! Pretty soon, the fog will lift in your life, and you're just liable to see some Dalmatian cows . . .

KISSES FROM HEAVEN

Let everything that has breath praise the Lord!
Praise the Lord!

Psalm 150:6 (ESV)

HEART TO HEAVEN

Father God, I praise You right now for who You are and all that You've done for me. You are an awesome God. Thank You, God, that You speak to us out of the mouths of babes. And, Lord, help me never to lose sight of the blessings in my life. In the mighty name of Jesus. Amen.

Chapter 36

NO HIDDEN PLACES

Recently, both of my girls were on college break at the same time, which rarely happens. Hearing their laughter coming from their bedrooms warmed my heart . . . and then I walked over to drop off their clean laundry, and my heart wasn't quite as warm. Their rooms looked like a tornado had blown through, more than once! That, too, brought back some memories of my girls and their messy rooms growing up—especially one particular time . . .

As I carried another load of dirty clothes to the laundry room, I glanced inside Abby's and Allyson's rooms. It was scary. Barbie dolls everywhere. Clothes and shoes all over the floor. Dresser drawers halfway open, with clothes spilling out of them. Candy bar wrappers scattered across their rooms. (Yes, my girls take after their mother and love their chocolate, too!)

It was ultimatum time.

"OK, here's the deal," I said to the girls, then ages 7 and 5. "You either clean up your rooms, or we're not going swimming today. That's final. Got it?"

"Yes, ma'am," Abby said, marching off to her room.

Allyson said nothing, following her older sister.

A few minutes later, Allyson bounded into the kitchen in her orange and yellow polka dot bathing suit and announced: "I'm finished!"

"Already finished cleaning your room?" I asked.

"Uh huh," she said, "come see."

To my amazement, her room looked really clean. Just as I was about to congratulate Allyson on her amazing cleaning abilities, she walked in front of her miniature recliner that sat in the corner and said, "Just don't look behind the chair."

Guilt was written all over her rosy little cheeks.

I had no choice. I had to look behind the recliner, and when I did, I saw a pile of clothes, several pairs of shoes, Barbie dolls, and candy wrappers. She was caught, and she knew it. Meanwhile, Abby had truly cleaned her room and was able to watch cartoons while Allyson had to put away the pile of stuff stacked behind her recliner. Ally whined and whimpered as she folded clothing, threw out trash, and put away dolls. Her little act of disobedience had cost us an hour of pool time. She was sorry, but being sorry couldn't get her back that hour she had lost. It was a good lesson for her, and a good lesson for me.

I thought about how many times in my life I had gone before the Father and said, "I'm finished cleaning up. Come and see, but just don't look behind that chair in the far corner of my heart."

Just like Allyson thought she could fool me, I thought I could fool God. And, just as Allyson's delayed obedience had cost her time at the pool, mine had kept me from walking in the fullness of God more than once. Every time I pull the old, "don't look behind the chair" routine, God just waits for me to repent, and then He puts me back on the right path as if I'd never missed a step. That's because He is so merciful and good. He will do the same for you. So, go ahead. Quit hiding those stinky, dirty, trashy, and sinful items from behind that chair in the corner of your heart, and let God help you make a clean start today. You don't need to hide anything from God. He knows everything anyway. Why not start clean today? God's waiting.

KISSES FROM HEAVEN

People who conceal their sins will not prosper,
but if they confess and turn from them,
they will receive mercy.

Proverbs 28:13 (NLT)

HEART TO HEAVEN

Lord, I am tired of hiding things from You. This very day, I give all of my heart to You—even the mess behind the chair in the corner of my heart. I ask that You help me move forward with You in total obedience and integrity, and help me to be a better mom. In the mighty name of Jesus, Amen.

Chapter 37

STAY NEAR TO HIM

"MOM!" Allyson, my then 5-year-old, shrieked.

I was in the process of making my mom's famous choc-olate oatmeal cookies when Ally screamed, causing me to dump the entire container of oats into the mixture . . . it only called for two cups.

It was one of those "mom cries" that sends mothers into an instant panic. I could tell her voice was coming from out-side, but I didn't see her out front when I peered through the dining room window.

"Mom, hurry!"

I ran to our backyard, scared that she might have fallen into our pool.

She wasn't there.

She must be in the front yard, I thought. *But where is she?*

Finally, I found her. She was way up in our live oak tree that stood in the far corner of our front yard . . . and she was stuck.

"Mom! Help me!"

I looked up at how high my baby girl had climbed and felt a little panic inside.

"Just a minute, babe," I called. "I'm coming."

Trying to remember how to climb a tree, I inched my way up—slowly, carefully, and prayerfully. Finally, I reached the branch directly beneath her and gently touched her leg closest to me.

"I'm going to reach up and place your foot next to me, Allyson, and I want you to carefully climb down to me."

"OK," she said through tears.

When she finally got close enough, she clung to me like she'd never clung before. Branch by branch, we proceeded down the tree, and the whole way down, she kept saying: "I'm sorry, Mommy. I'm sorry, Mommy. I'm sorry, Mommy."

Once we were safely on the ground, I reminded Allyson that she wouldn't have been stuck in our tree if she'd been obedient. After all, she wasn't supposed to go outside by herself, and she certainly wasn't supposed to climb our tall tree—not without help. Allyson wiped her tears on her Tweety Bird shirt, said she was sorry, and promised she'd never do it again, and then ran inside to watch cartoons with her sister. As I dusted myself off and headed back to the kitchen to scoop the extra oats out of my batter, I couldn't help thinking about Ally's traumatic tree experience and how much it reminded me of my own walk with God at various times in my life.

Maybe you can relate, as well.

We do our own thing, act in disobedience, and when we get stuck in a scary tall tree, we holler, "Help, God, and hurry!" After He rescues us, we cling to Him, crying and saying how sorry we are, until we're safely on solid ground. Then, we go about our own lives until we need Him again.

Wouldn't it be better if we stayed close to God *all* the time—not just when we get into trouble? Then we wouldn't have to holler for Him because He'd already be there. Though we often get upset with our children for making poor decisions and directly disobeying us, isn't it ironic how often we do the same thing with our Heavenly Father?

It seems that as we parent our children, God is parenting us. I'm so thankful that God is a God of mercy and grace and that His mercies are new every morning because I've been stuck in a tall tree more times than I care to admit. How about you?

Let's determine today to follow God and His ways and set a good example for our children. And, let's draw near to God because the Bible tells us if we'll draw near to Him, He will draw near to us (James 4:8).

KISSES FROM HEAVEN

God is our refuge and strength,
an ever-present help in trouble.

Psalm 46:1 (NIV)

HEART TO HEAVEN

Father, help me to stay near You all the time—not just in times of trouble. And, Lord, help me to be more patient with my children when they disobey the same way You show me grace when I do the same. In the mighty name of Jesus, Amen.

Chapter 38

PINK BLANKET CRISIS

"No!" Allyson, my then 2-year-old screamed at her older sister Abby.

"That's mine!" she continued, jerking her white, silky blanket out of Abby's grip. "Miiiiiiiine!"

Abby immediately burst into tears, dropping to the floor in complete desperation. She apparently couldn't find her favorite blanket, and her sister wouldn't share hers. Before I could intervene, the real fit began. Abby rolled from one side of the hallway to the other, screaming and breathing irregularly with each roll.

"Where's my blankie? Where's my blankie?" she continued her tirade.

Abby had lost her pink blanket, and now Allyson had reclaimed her white one. In her 3-year-old reasoning, Abby believed that her happy, seemingly go-lucky life was over.

She didn't think she could possibly go on without her pink blankie.

You might say she overreacted a bit.

"Ab, have some chocolate milk while Mommy helps you find your blankie," I comforted.

She wanted nothing to do with me or her favorite treat of all time—"chockie milk."

I absolutely could not console her. So, I stepped over my traumatized toddler on a quest to find her beloved blanket. After looking in all of the usual spots, I noticed a ragged pink corner sticking out from under a pile of stuffed animals in the corner of Abby's room. After a quick tug on the pink corner, the blanket mystery was solved.

I walked back into where Abby lay, curled up into a sobbing ball of pitifulness, and said, "Look what Mommy found!"

Abby looked up through teary eyes and gazed at her long, lost friend.

"My blankie!" she shrieked, ever so excited. "You saved me, Mommy."

With that, she jumped up, grabbed the blanket, and took her place next to Allyson, who was already watching Barney and Baby Bop on TV.

Her pink blanket was back, and all was well in the world.

Abby's major overreaction made me think—I, too, have

had many "pink blanket crises" in my life. Something rather insignificant will go wrong, and, suddenly, my world is destroyed. I cry and mope and pout and have a few temper tantrums, and then God will reveal the very simple solution that I would have seen earlier if I had not overreacted so badly. I find that I often do that when it comes to my children. While I can be a bit more rational and patient with adverse situations in my own life, I get really frustrated and overreact when something goes wrong in my children's lives. Like when someone treats one of my girls unfairly—my mama bear instincts take over, and I sometimes have a major overreaction. Before I can calm myself down and see the situation through rational eyes, I've hollered, acted awful, and chewed out every person I feel has wronged my babies.

In the aftermath, God always gets my attention, and I realize that I've overreacted and usually have to say a few "I'm sorrys" before all is right in my world again.

Maybe you can relate.

How many times have you let a pink blanket crisis overwhelm you, throwing you into a blue funk? It doesn't have to be that way. If we will keep our eyes fixed on Jesus, He will make sure we find our "pink blankets" every time—in His time. As we draw closer to Him, we will become more like Him and have fewer pink blanket meltdowns. And, before long, we'll be quicker at recognizing when we're about to have a pink blanket breakdown and, like Abby, we'll be able to look to the Father and say, "You saved me!"

KISSES FROM HEAVEN

Let us fix our eyes on Jesus, the author and perfecter of our faith, who for the joy set before him endured the cross.

Hebrews 12:2 (NIV)

HEART TO HEAVEN

Father, help me to keep my eyes on You and not on the "pink blanket crises" that try to overwhelm me and steal my joy. Lord, please temper my "mama bear" instinct when it comes to situations with my children, and help me to react with love and mercy, the way that You would have me to behave. In the mighty name of Jesus, Amen.

Chapter 39

IT'S OK, MOMMY

The yard of our new Texas home needed a lot of attention, but we were determined to turn the tundra into lush, green grass. Jeff began trimming the overgrown hedges, while the girls and I started picking up the large sticks and debris. After an hour or so, I escaped inside for a Diet Coke and Snickers break. Moments later, my then 4-year-old Allyson bolted into the house.

"It bit me! It bit me!" she screamed.

"What bit you?"

"I don't know but it hurt!" she continued.

I knelt down and inspected Ally's right calf. There was a red, raised bump but nothing too terrible-looking.

"I think you're going to live," I teased. "Probably just a fire ant."

I put some bug-bite ointment on the red bump and kissed Ally on the head.

As I gave Allyson her bath that night, I noticed the red bump had become a little larger, but it didn't look alarming. So, I put some more ointment on it and put her to bed.

The next morning, I was awakened by the sunlight spilling in through our bedroom blinds.

It's going to be a beautiful day, I thought.

Then my eyes glanced at the alarm clock. It read, "7:35."

"7:35! Oh my gosh! Jeff, we overslept!"

The morning was a blur. I dropped the girls off at school, drove like a mad woman to work, and rushed inside my office at 8:32—only two minutes late.

Just as I sat down into my office chair, the phone rang.

Oh no, I thought. *My boss must've noticed I came in a little late.*

"Hello," I said, sheepishly.

"Mrs. Adams, I am calling about Allyson," said the voice on the other end of the line. "Were you aware that Allyson has a very serious bite on her right leg?"

I realized in all of the confusion, I hadn't even looked at her leg that morning.

"It looks a lot like a wound from a brown recluse spider," she continued. "I don't say that to scare you, but I think she needs immediate medical attention."

Minutes later, I was at Ally's school. The bite was no longer red; it had turned dark, almost black in color, surrounded by a perfect circle of purplish-red.

I started to panic.

I called a nearby pediatrician, described Allyson's wound, and told the nurse we were on our way. Then, I called Jeff and my mother and blubbered a few minutes to each of them. All the while, Allyson sat quietly in the backseat.

My sobbing was interrupted by a sweet little voice from the backseat.

"It's OK, Mommy, I already prayed about my leg."

Amazed, I looked at her through my rearview mirror.

Allyson had peace because she had already given the situation to the Father. At age 4, she knew the most important thing to do in a crisis—pray. I, then 29 years old, had totally missed it.

Allyson remained calm throughout the hysterical outbursts of her mother, the poking and prodding of the doctor and nurses, the injection of medicine into her leg—all of it. I finally calmed down once I heard the doctor say, "She is going to be just fine. Just watch the wound overnight and bring her back tomorrow for another shot."

I nodded, thanked the doctor, and hugged Allyson so hard she said, "ouch."

Allyson's leg took a few weeks to heal, but eventually,

all signs of the bite disappeared; however, memories of that insect incident will stick with me forever.

Allyson taught me a great lesson that day—go to God first. Prayer should always be our first instinct. We shouldn't be too proud to learn from our children. Out of the mouths of babes, right?

KISSES FROM HEAVEN

Out of the mouth of babes and nursing infants
You have ordained strength,
Because of Your enemies,
That You may silence the enemy and the avenger.
Psalm 8:2 (NKJV)

HEART TO HEAVEN

Father, help me to not be too prideful to learn from my children. Thank You for teaching me through them. And, help me, Lord, to always make You my first option. In the mighty name of Jesus, Amen.

Chapter 40

BEING TOOTHLESS ISN'T SO BAD

"Stop it, Ally! It's not funny!"

"Is so!" Allyson, my then 5-year-old, taunted.

The unpleasant exchange was followed by bursts of squeals and crying. I peered out from beneath my pillow and looked at the alarm clock through squinted eyes. It was time to get up anyway. Rolling out of bed, I slipped on my leopard print slippers and stumbled down the hallway toward the girls' rooms.

"What's going on?" I demanded.

"Ally is making fun of my loose tooth," Abby, my then first-grader, whined.

"Is that true, Allyson?"

She said nothing, indicating her guilt.

"Ally, it isn't nice to make fun of people," I reminded. "Tell Abby you're sorry."

"Sorry," Allyson said, with just a twinge of "I'm saying it but I don't really mean it" in her voice.

Abby was satisfied with the apology, and that was good enough for me. Besides, I had breakfast to fix. As I hurried into the kitchen, Jeff passed me in the hall, giving me a quick goodbye kiss on his way out.

"I'll pull that tooth for you tonight," Daddy called to Abby who was wiggling her loose tooth.

"NO!" Abby hollered. "I don't want you to."

It was Abby's very first loose tooth, and she wanted to hang onto that tooth as long as possible.

Days passed and that poor, little tooth hung on for dear life. Abby was obsessed with it. She carefully avoided the loose tooth while brushing her teeth. She refused to eat anything that required much chewing. And, she was constantly wiggling it with her tongue.

Then, one night as I was loading the dishwasher I heard, "My tooth! My tooth! MOM!!"

I dashed down the hall and into Abby's room. There she stood, smiling a toothless grin and holding a sucker with a tooth stuck to it. It had fought a good fight, but that little tooth lost to a chocolate Tootsie Roll pop.

That night, Abby tucked the tooth under her pillow and

a tooth fairy wearing leopard-print slippers delivered the cash. The following day, Abby was inducted into her school's "Lost Tooth Club" and received a special sticker in honor of the important occasion.

Funny, isn't it?

Abby was so afraid to lose that first tooth. She tried everything to keep that old, baby tooth in place. But, when the tooth finally lost out to a lollipop, Abby was thrilled to see it go because of all the benefits that accompanied the monumental event.

I later thought about Abby's loose-tooth experience, and realized God wanted me to learn a lesson from that experience, too. He gently pointed out I had some "loose teeth" in my life—things I was holding back from Him. I imagine Abby was afraid to lose her tooth, fearing she would have a toothless smile forever. Besides, her old tooth was so comfortable. She had grown used to it. She was afraid she'd miss it.

I had held onto the "loose teeth" in my spiritual life for the same reasons.

But, you know what? When I finally let loose of those things in my life, God replaced them with better, stronger, and more beautiful ones—just like Abby's beautiful, white permanent tooth replaced the old, weakened baby one.

Permanent teeth are a sign of maturity. So, I have a question for you: how are your spiritual teeth? If you resemble

Snaggletooth, or if you're still walking around with a mouth-ful of worn-out baby teeth, it's time to let go and let God. It's time to join the "Lost Tooth Club" and enjoy the benefits of membership. Trust me, God gives a lot better rewards than that leopard-print slipper-wearing Tooth Fairy.

KISSES FROM HEAVEN

Do not be anxious about anything, but in everything by prayer and supplication with thanksgiving let your requests be made known to God.

Philippians 4:6 (ESV)

HEART TO HEAVEN

Father, help me to trust You more and be willing and obedient to turn everything in my life over to You—my hopes, my dreams, my marriage, and my children. I love You so much. In the mighty name of Jesus, Amen.

CHOCOLATE-COVERED CONVERSATION HEARTS...

SPEAKING INTO THE LIVES OF YOUR CHILDREN

MY AUNT MARY ANN FLEETWOOD

Mary Ann has been friends with Martha Savage since they were little girls, and one of the wonderful memories she has from all the time spent at Martha's house was eating the delicious chocolate spice cake that Martha's mom, Ruth, always made.

"It was this chocolate spice cake," Mary Ann said. "Ruth called it the Chocolate Depression Cake because the recipe didn't call for any eggs. I guess eggs were hard to come by in those days."

Eventually, Mary Ann got the recipe from Ruth and started making the cake, too. Well, it was such a hit with Mary Ann's family, that any time there was a birthday, she'd have to make a Chocolate Spice Cake. That tradition continues today.

Mary Ann made one addition to the recipe—she added some rich icing at the request of her children and grandchildren, but the cake is good with or without the icing, according to Mary Ann.

CHOCOLATE SPICE CAKE

1½ cups flour

1 cup sugar

1 tablespoon cocoa

1 cup of sour milk (buttermilk)

½ cup of butter or Crisco

1 teaspoon nutmeg

1 teaspoon cinnamon

1 teaspoon baking soda

Sift all dry ingredients and mix together. Cream butter (or shortening) and sugar together in a separate bowl; add milk alternately. Next, add the dry ingredients to the butter mixture a little at a time until well blended. Bake at 350° for 45 minutes or until the sides start to pull away from the pan.

Best Chocolate Icing I've Ever Tasted!:

⅓ cup whole milk

½ cup semi-sweet chocolate morsels

¾ cup sugar

1 teaspoon vanilla

1 tablespoon of butter

Bring the ingredients to a rolling boil stirring constantly; While still hot, beat it until it is of a spreading consistency. Once the cake has cooled, add your icing.

Chapter 41

DON'T BE A STUPID HEAD!

We had just experienced a wonderful service at Eagle Mountain International Church in Fort Worth, Texas, about the power of our words. As we loaded the girls into our SUV, they were already fussing at one another. I tried to ignore their bickering, still replaying Pastor George's message in my head and heart. We hadn't taken the girls to children's service that morning, electing to let them stay in "big service" with us. I thought they had just been coloring and playing dolls during church, but I soon discovered they had actually been listening.

"You're a stupid head," 6-year-old Abby said to her little sister. "Ally is a stupid head. Ally is a stupid head."

Just as I was about to intervene, Ally blurted out, "Mom, Abby is making bad confessions over me."

Jeff and I both tried to choke back laughter at Ally's very accurate comment. Our little 4-year-old daughter understood the power of words that day, and she didn't want her big sister saying anything negative about her. Apparently, Pastor George's message had made an impact on little Allyson, as well.

Proverbs 18:21 says the tongue holds the power of life and death. The Scriptures also say that the tongue, though it is a small part of the human body, can make great boasts and cause immense damage. If you've ever been on the receiving end of hurtful words, you know the full meaning of that Scripture.

"Words both challenge and change us. Words deeply affect us. An unruly and unkind tongue can wound us," explained Paul F. Davis, a worldwide minister and author of *Breakthrough for a Broken Heart.* "That being said, anything spoken to you contrary to the Word of God can be discarded as you renew your mind according to Scripture."

That's what I've had to do when hurtful words have been said to me, and that's what you'll have to do if you're still stinging from cutting comments in your past.

We need to learn to combat negative words with God's Word. If someone says, "You are a bad mother," don't think on that untruth. Instead, remind yourself what God says about you. He says, "You are the head and not the tail. You are an overcomer! You can do all things through Christ who gives you strength."

Not only can others' words deeply affect us, but also our words can deeply affect others. What are you saying to your family? Do you build up with your words, or do you tear down?

Taming the tongue begins with controlling your emotions and allowing God to fill you up with His love because our words essentially are an overflow of what lives in our hearts. If your heart is full of love, peace, joy, contentment, grace, and self-control, then your mouth will be full of the same.

Practice building up your spouse and children this week. Here are a few phrases to get you started:

- I love you more than a double-dipped chocolate covered peanut!
- You make my life happier just by being in it.
- I not only love you, but also I believe in you.
- You have special qualities that no one else has.
- You can do it!
- You are a gift from God!
- I am so thankful for you.
- You are a bright spot in my life.

Take every opportunity to use your words to encourage and uplift your family, and don't say ugly things in jest, thinking it's OK. It's never OK, and to quote Abby, that makes you "a stupid head." Don't be "a stupid head"; be an encourager instead!

KISSES FROM HEAVEN

Let no corrupting talk come out of your mouths, but only such as is good for building up, as fits the occasion, that it may give grace to those who hear.
Ephesians 4:29 (ESV)

HEART TO HEAVEN

God, please help me to use my words to speak life and love into my family. In the mighty name of Jesus, Amen.

Chapter 42

SPEAK THE WORD

Do you ever feel like the words of wisdom you speak into your children's lives are often ignored? I think all moms have felt like that at one time or another—especially when our children are tweens and teens—but more is sinking in than we realize.

I found that out, quite by accident one afternoon.

As I was dropping off laundry in the girls' rooms, I overheard my then 16-year-old daughter, Abby, and her best friend chit chatting quite loudly. I was about to burst in the room and suggest some chocolate ice cream and a chick flick, when I realized that they were talking seriously. This was not their normal, "who is going out with who" conversation.

"You have no idea what I've been going through," her friend shouted. "My family is totally falling apart, so don't tell me that God gives a crap about me!"

Her friend was sobbing, so much so, that I was truly concerned and wondered if I should pop in and see if I could do anything to help. But then I heard Abby boldly say: "Just because you can't see or feel God doesn't mean He isn't working. You just have to trust Him and know that He won't let you down. That's what faith is all about—believing before you see it."

I wanted to drop the laundry basket, flip it over, stand up on it, and applaud Abby. I was so proud of her for wisely counseling her frustrated friend, and I was so relieved to know that the Word we had spoken into her hadn't fallen on deaf ears. She not only had heard it; she'd believed it and was now preaching it! I am so thankful the Lord allowed me to overhear her that day because I often thought back to her faith-filled words whenever it seemed that Abby was moving down the wrong path during that next year of high school. About the time I'd think, *She is making the wrong decision. She's not listening to us. She isn't living for God. She knows better* . . . God would bring her words back to my remembrance: "Just because you can't see or feel God doesn't mean he isn't working . . . " I was sure that God was doing a work in Abby's life—I just couldn't always see evidence of that work. But He was, and He continues to work in both of my daughters' lives, and in mine.

So, let me encourage you today—keep speaking the Word into the lives of your kiddos, even if it seems like they aren't getting it. Keep pointing out the everyday miracles to them because they may act uninterested, but they're listening. Keep taking advantage of those "teachable moments," and sharing words of wisdom even if it seems like they are completely tuning you out because they really aren't. The Bible assures us that God's Word never returns void, so rest on that promise today. And, remember, they're not only listening, they're observing so make sure you walk the talk. As they see you living for God and walking in love, day in and day out, they will be impacted for the Kingdom.

KISSES FROM HEAVEN

*As the rain and the snow come down from
heaven, and do not return to it without watering
the earth and making it bud and flourish, so that
it yields seed for the sower and bread for the eater,
so is my word that goes out from my mouth:
It will not return to me empty, but will
accomplish what I desire and achieve
the purpose for which I sent it.*

Isaiah 55:10-11 (NIV)

HEART TO HEAVEN

God, please help me speak the Word into my children's lives at every opportunity. And, Father, I pray that their hearts would be ready to receive it. And, Lord, please help me to not just talk the talk but to walk the walk so that I might be a good witness to my children. In the mighty name of Jesus, Amen.

Chapter 43

NO FREE WORDS

I love the movie *You've Got Mail* starring Meg Ryan as Kathleen Kelly and Tom Hanks as Joe Fox, don't you? (Who doesn't love watching a good romantic comedy with a box of Junior Mints and large Diet Coke?) *You've Got Mail* is one of my all-time favorites, but there's one scene that really speaks to me. In this particular clip, Kathleen is frustrated that she can never say the exact thing she wants to say at the moment of confrontation. She always thinks of the perfect comeback hours later, which, of course, does her no good because the moment has passed. On the other hand, Joe is able to say cutting comebacks without any hesitation. She e-mails him, saying that she wishes she had that ability, and Joe tells her that he wishes he could give her his talent because it's dangerous. He goes on to explain that saying exactly what you think, exactly when you think it, almost always leads to guilt and regret. Later in the film when Kathleen is able to say the cruelest comments right on cue, she realizes the truth in her friend's e-mail. She feels badly for her hurtful words, but she can't take them back. The damage has been done.

I can so relate to Kathleen Kelly in this movie, how about you?

Have you ever snapped and said something to your children that you wish you hadn't? I wish I could say I haven't, but I'd be lying if I did. One particular time that stands out in my mind happened when I was helping Abby and Allyson with their tumbling passes for their upcoming middle school cheer tryouts. Practice wasn't going exactly as planned, and Abby was becoming more frustrated by the minute. She had thrown a gorgeous round-off back handspring, back tuck the week before at gymnastics class, but fear was getting the best of her and she simply wouldn't throw it that afternoon. Ally, on the other hand, had no fear—ever! She threw tumbling passes and stunts that she probably shouldn't have!

I had tried the encouraging approach, saying: "You can do it, Abby! Just throw it! You've got this!" But she wouldn't do it. She would run down the gym floor; do a round-off, and stop. She did this over and over until she had worked herself into a tizzy. Meanwhile, Ally was flipping all over the gym, about to wear herself out, throwing tumbling pass after tumbling pass.

I thoughtlessly said, "Abby, your technique is way better than Ally's, and yet she is out tumbling you every pass. You're a much better tumbler than Ally, but you're just a fraidy cat."

With one stupid statement, I had crippled their confidence and caused strife between sisters. All Abby heard was that she was a fraidy cat, and all Ally heard was that her older sister was a much better tumbler than she was. I so wanted to retract my words, but the damage was already done. Sure, I said I was sorry—because I was! But, it took quite a while before they recovered from those hurtful words I'd said. Even though my intentions were not to hurt my girls, that didn't make their pain any less real.

That's the thing about words; they do damage immediately. And even when you say you're sorry, their sting remains. So, think before you speak. Do whatever it takes to keep the cutting comments from escaping your mouth. Bite your tongue if you have to; just don't say the first thing that pops into your head without thinking through the consequences of your words. You may have a sore tongue, but your heart will feel good!

Learn from my mistake and use your mouth to encourage, not condemn. There is much power in words, so let's use that power for good!

KISSES FROM HEAVEN

A soft answer turns away wrath,
but a harsh word stirs up anger.

Proverbs 15:1 (NKJV)

HEART TO HEAVEN

God, please help me to think before I speak. Keep a watch over my mouth, Heavenly Father, so that I only speak words of edification. In the mighty name of Jesus, Amen.

Chapter 44

ARE YOU LISTENING?

We've raised our girls in church. They know all of the Bible stories. They understand the concepts of healing, faith, sowing and reaping, tithing, and so on. But, I didn't just want them to know about God—I wanted them to *know* God. And, that only comes from spending time in His presence. Both of my girls, at different times in their lives, have asked me how to hear from God. I remember Abby asked once, "Like, how do you know if it's really God you're hearing from or just your own mind thinking thoughts?"

Good question.

I've had that same question posed to me when I minister at churches across the country, and my answer is always the same: "Stay tuned into God all the time, and you will hear from Him. The Bible says we should pray without ceasing, so do that. Keep that line of communication open 24/7. He will direct your steps because Proverbs 3:5-6 assures us of that."

As moms, isn't that reassuring? God wants to speak to us and lead us. All we have to do is seek Him. Now, He may not speak in that big, booming Charlton Heston kind of voice, but He will get His message across—sometimes in the most unexpected of ways. That's exactly what happened to my daughter Allyson's best friend, Wesley.

A full-time college student, Wes also works nights for an electrician. During the fall of last year, Wes had been working at an elementary school in southern Indiana. Every day, he would walk up and down the hallways en route to replace another light, passing many decorated bulletin boards along the way. But on this particular day, one of the decorations caught his attention.

Gerald the Giraffe had this to say: "If you find someone who makes you smile, who checks up on you often to see if you're okay, who watches out for you and wants the very best for you, don't let them go. Keep them close and don't take them for granted. People like that are hard to find."

Woven into Gerald the Giraffe's observation was the exact confirmation that Wesley had been seeking. Wes shared this testimony on social media, and he gave me permission to share it with you.

He wrote:

I've been <u>praying</u> a lot lately, asking God for a little bit of guidance, and this little quote just struck a chord in my heart . . . I haven't always lived my life by this, and I know for a fact that I've taken some people just like this for granted.

But thankfully our God is a God of second chances, and a lot of them have stuck around through everything. So next time God brings someone like this into your life, just remember what Gerald the Giraffe says.

Precious.

I'm sure that "Gerald the Giraffe quote" had been hanging in that same spot for weeks, but on the day that Wesley prayed for guidance about a certain situation in his life, God caused him to notice that quote, and it brought a sense of overwhelming peace and direction to his life.

I love that, don't you?

So, if you're truly seeking wisdom and direction from God, He will find a way to speak to you. Sometimes, a Scripture you've read a million times will practically jump off the pages of your Bible, providing the insight you need that very day. Other times, God will use a friend, a family member, your children, a printed message on the inside of a Dove chocolate wrapper, or even Gerald the Giraffe to speak to your heart.

Be aware of God's leading and receptive to his guidance, and you just might have your "Gerald the Giraffe" moment today, tomorrow, or when you most need it.

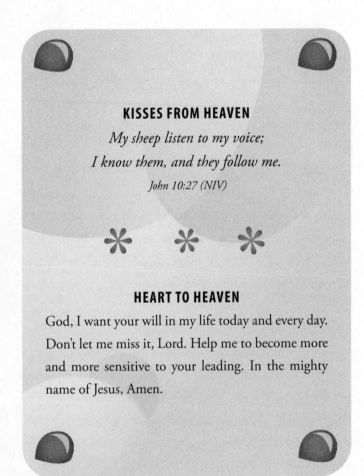

KISSES FROM HEAVEN

My sheep listen to my voice;
I know them, and they follow me.
John 10:27 (NIV)

HEART TO HEAVEN

God, I want your will in my life today and every day. Don't let me miss it, Lord. Help me to become more and more sensitive to your leading. In the mighty name of Jesus, Amen.

Chapter 45

OPEN THIS WHEN . . .

It's true we live in a day and age where an actual handwritten note is sort of a lost art form. Teens who have grown up sending texts and emails and Facebook messages find it "old-fashioned" to write a note on paper. Adults are guilty of this, too, because it's simply more convenient to send a quick text or shoot an email to your spouse, sister, child, or best friend. But a handwritten note means so much more.

In a recent *Wall Street Journal* article on "The Lost Art of the Handwritten Note," author Philip Hensher shares how our increasing reliance on typing and texting is making the handwritten note about as relevant as the fax machine. He says, "The ready communication through electronic means that has replaced the handwritten letter is wonderful. But we have definitely lost something here, and those Skype, email and text exchanges won't be treasured in the way that my teenage letters, scribbled journals and postcards have been for years."

Hensher raises a good point—there's simply nothing like a lovely, handwritten, thoughtful note. It seems I'm not the only one who agrees with Hensher. Recently, I've noticed that handwritten letters are back en vogue via a movement called, "Open When . . . " envelopes. The premise is this: you write letters for various occasions such as "Open When You're Feeling Sad," "Open When You're Missing Me," "Open When You Need Encouragement," "Open When You're Mad at Me," "Open When You Need to Know How Awesome You Are," "Open When You Can't Sleep," etc. And, inside each envelope is a handwritten note featuring inside jokes, shared memories, favorite quotes, and other inspiring tidbits. People personalize the envelopes with stickers, glitter, photographs, Hershey Kisses and other decorations.

How do I know so much about this trend? Well, I watched with great pride as both of my daughters crafted personal, heartfelt letters to their long-time boyfriends. And, both of their boyfriends were deeply touched by their presents of prose. Abby's boyfriend joked, "I might need another 'Open When You're Mad At Me' letter because I've pretty much worn that one out." But in all seriousness, these young men so appreciated the time and effort and sincerity of each letter.

There's just something special about the written word, isn't there? I remember one Christmas when money was tight, my husband and I opted not to buy each other any gifts. Instead, Jeff wrote me a two-page letter. It wasn't decorated with stickers, glitter, or pictures. It wasn't placed in a fancy envelope. It was written on notebook paper and stuffed into a plain white envelope. In fact, he had even scratched out some words and written other words above them throughout the letter, but I loved every word and every scribble. Why? Because they were precious words, sweet memories, and heartfelt confessions from my one true love. It's one of the nicest gifts I've ever received, and it was paired with a giant Hershey Kiss—what's not to love?

All of this letter writing got me to thinking, God has written an entire Bible full of love letters to us. The Bible is also filled with precious promises, words of hope, words of wisdom, and the answers to any question we'll ever have. It's the best "Mom Manual" you could ever have. And, it's the original "Open When . . . " letter because no matter what we're feeling or what we're in need of, the Bible contains the very life-filled words we need.

So, here's what I challenge you to do this week. Make time to read the Word of God every single day. Secondly, write letters to your children and your spouse. They don't have to be of the "Open When . . . " variety, and they don't have to be elaborately decorated. They simply have to be heartfelt and handwritten.

As moms, our words are powerful, so use them wisely.

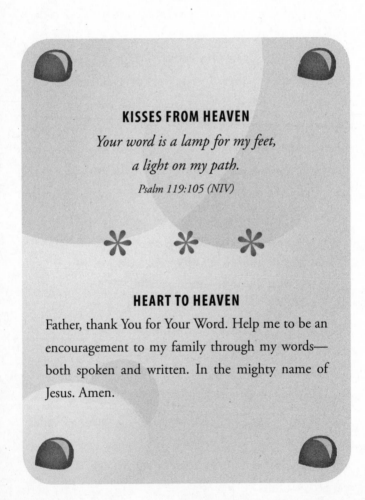

KISSES FROM HEAVEN

Your word is a lamp for my feet,
a light on my path.
Psalm 119:105 (NIV)

✳ ✳ ✳

HEART TO HEAVEN

Father, thank You for Your Word. Help me to be an encouragement to my family through my words—both spoken and written. In the mighty name of Jesus. Amen.

TRANSITIONS, TEARS, AND TURTLES . . .

TRUSTING GOD THROUGH ALL OF LIFE'S CHANGES

MY SISTER-IN-LAW BARB MEDLOCK

I was in first grade when my brother Rob first brought Barb home to meet the fam, and I have loved her from day one. When Barb married my brother, she immediately fit right into our family. Turns out, she didn't really like to cook, either. (lol) She and my brother have four amazing children: Meghan, Jay, Mindy, and Jon, affectionately referred to as "The Cleveland Medlock Bunch"—we just wish they lived a little closer to us. But, when they do come to visit, Barb better come bearing "Reindeer Mix" because it's a Medlock family fave!

While the "Reindeer Mix" name indicates you only make this scrumptious snack mix at Christmas, we find it's great for Super Bowl parties, NCAA Final Four shindigs, Euchre tournaments, and pretty much any family reunion. It's easy, and it's so yummy! (I actually made this one recently!)

REINDEER MIX

1 pound of white almond bark or white chocolate chips

1 tablespoon of vegetable oil

3 cups of Corn Chex

3 cups of Rice Chex

3 cups of Cheerios

1 cup of dry roasted nuts

½ pound of plain M&Ms

½ pound of thin pretzels (broken up)

Melt white bark on low. Add 1 tablespoon of oil. Mix well and pour over cereal, nuts, M&Ms, and pretzels. Mix well and set on parchment paper. Then, put it in a big tin and enjoy!

Chapter 46

GIVE YOUR CHILDREN THE BEST GIFT

Our ladies Bible study leader asked us, "Besides the knowledge of Jesus, what's the greatest gift you can give your children?" There were a lot of really good answers given, and no real "right or wrong" response, but not one of us gave the answer she was after, which was surprising.

"A truly happy home—a home where you and your spouse love, honor, and respect each other," she shared. "That's the response I was hoping you'd give."

I thought that was powerful, and her words made me take a good, hard look at my marriage that day. Truly, that was the beginning of a new era in mine and Jeff's relationship. Though my marriage isn't perfect today, it's pretty wonderful; however, it wasn't always so great. We've had our "seasons of sticking it out" simply because we promised we would on our wedding day almost 24 years ago. You know when it became more wonderful? When I finally put into practice what my Bible study leader taught me that day about honoring my husband. It completely transformed our home. I kept praying for God to change him; turns out, I was the biggest part of the problem.

Whether you're in a loveless marriage, or your marriage isn't as wonderful as it used to be, or you're a single mom hoping to find the man of your dreams, this nugget of truth is for you. If you'll let your man know that you are in his corner, adoring him, he will think you are the most beautiful woman in the world and love you like crazy. Trust me!

Statistician and author Shaunti Feldhahn polled 1,000 men for her book, *For Women Only: What You Need to Know About the Inner Lives of Men,* so that we could better understand the men God has given us to love. When polled concerning their favorite movie scene of all time, the men overwhelmingly chose a scene from a baseball movie. You might be thinking that most men would've chosen a shoot 'em up clip from some action-adventure movie. Not so. The most popular scene—the scene that evoked the greatest emotion from these 1,000 men—came from *The Natural.* Remember that one, starring Robert Redford?

The scene goes something like this: Robert Redford is pitching, and the crowd is booing him and berating him.

Redford steps off the mound and looks into the hostile crowd until his eyes lock on a woman, his gal, his love. She is quietly standing in support of him, smiling with her eyes. In the midst of the chaos and screaming, he finds peace and strength and confidence simply by knowing she is in his corner, loving him and being proud of him.

That's what our men want. They want to know that we love them and support them, no matter what. They want to know that we still think they've "got it going on." They want to know that we're proud of them. You say, "But, Michelle, I do think that. My husband knows I love him." Maybe he does, but maybe he needs to hear it more often. Or maybe he needs to hear less criticism from you. Or maybe he just needs to know that you support him and appreciate all that he does for you and the family.

See, if we honor and adore the men God has placed in our lives, they'll love us like we need and desire to be loved, and our marriages will become stronger and happier. And, in turn, our homes will be happier, too. So, go ahead. Give your children a wonderful gift—a gift that is even better than chocolate—I promise.

KISSES FROM HEAVEN

The same goes for you wives: Be good wives to your husbands, responsive to their needs . . . Cultivate inner beauty, the gentle, gracious kind that God delights in.

1 Peter 3:1-4 (MSG)

HEART TO HEAVEN

God, please help me to love my husband and honor him the way You would have me to, and let our love create a wonderful environment for our children to thrive. In the mighty name of Jesus, Amen.

Chapter 47

WHY'D WE HAVE TO MOVE?

I will never *get unpacked*, I thought as I stood in the hot garage of our newly acquired Texas home.

It was our first big move. Jeff and I had lived in the same small southern Indiana town our entire lives. We were high school sweethearts, dating off and on for seven years, before marrying right after college.

In those seven years of marriage, we had moved into our first home, had two children, become active in our home church, and worked in the community that had always been so good to us. (Did I mention that my parents lived next door?) Our roots ran very deep, so moving meant tremendous upheaval in our lives, yet we knew in our hearts that God was leading us to Fort Worth, Texas.

It was scary.

Weeks later as I unpacked the last box, I sighed with

relief. The house was actually coming together. I had started to like our new Texas home. I even bought a pair of cowboy boots, just so I'd feel a little more local.

As I carried the empty box to the roadside for trash pick-up, I noticed Abby sitting on the curb, playing in a small mound of sand.

"How's it going, Ab?" I called.

"Terrible," she grumbled.

I walked over and plopped down right beside her.

"What seems to be the trouble?" I asked, trying to be upbeat.

"Everything."

"Anything I can do?"

"Yeah," she said, "you could move us back to Indiana."

That's when I realized that Abby wasn't adjusting as well as I'd hoped.

"I hate it here. Why'd we have to move? There's no park. We don't have a swing set, and I miss Mamaw and Papaw and Nana and Granddad."

"I know," I comforted, pulling her close to me. "I miss them, too."

"Why can't it be the way it used to be? I want my old life back!" Abby cried, running into the house.

As I watched Abby in so much pain, I hurt for her. I knew some of what she was experiencing because I was going through the same emotions. She just couldn't understand how anything good could ever come of our move. There were days when I wondered that myself, but I could see the big picture with the help of God's binoculars. Abby could only see one thing—her world was radically different—and she didn't like it one bit.

Almost a year after moving into our Texas home, Abby was invited to a sleepover at a classmate's house. I was sure she'd be excited about going, but she seemed quite apathetic about the whole thing. As I folded her Scooby Doo nightgown and placed it neatly inside her polka-dot suitcase, Ab dove onto her bed and announced, "I'm not going."

"Why not?" I asked.

"Because I like being home," she said, matter-of-factly. "You wanna watch a movie with me tonight?"

"Sure," I said, smiling.

It was the first time Abby had shown any affection for our new home. In fact, I think it was the first time she'd even referred to our Texas residence as *home*. Ab had finally realized that "home" had little to do with where we were geographically located. It had much more to do with where we spent time together—watching movies, eating chocolate pudding, painting toenails, playing with our puppies, and simply being a family.

It's been decades since that first move, and since then,

we've survived another cross-country family move back to Indiana, as well as moves to different colleges in Kentucky, Florida, and California. Each move had its own set of exciting and sometimes scary circumstances, but we all learned that home is truly where you make it, and God always goes with you.

KISSES FROM HEAVEN

Have I not commanded you? Be strong and courageous. Do not be afraid; do not be discouraged, for the Lord your God will be with you wherever you go.

Joshua 1:9 (NIV)

HEART TO HEAVEN

God, please help me to always use You as my compass and to remember that You go with me wherever I go. In the mighty name of Jesus, Amen.

Chapter 48

WHICH SHOE GOES ON WHICH FOOT?

Just as we were rushing out the door on one of those marathon mornings, I realized that Allyson was still carrying around her pink sparkly tennis shoes.

"Why aren't your shoes on your feet?" I asked.

"Because you didn't tell me which shoe goes on which foot!"

"Remember what Daddy taught you?" I asked. "You match the curve of the shoe with the curve of your foot. That's how you tell which shoe goes on which foot."

She nodded as if she understood. I felt we'd made some sort of breakthrough.

After school, we headed to McDonald's Playland for some dinner and fun.

After wolfing down their Happy Meals, the girls slipped off their shoes and disappeared inside the brightly-colored tunnels. I finished my chocolate shake and read the newspaper to catch up on what was going on in the world beyond elementary school.

The next 45 minutes flew by!

"ABBY and ALLYSON!!" I called to the little faces looking at me from a window in one of the tunnels. "C'mon, we've got to get home."

Abby quickly slipped on her sandals, while Allyson studied her shoes for several minutes. First she'd take a shoe and hold it up next to her foot, checking the curves to see if they matched. Then, she'd take the other shoe and do the same.

Finally, in total frustration, Allyson asked, "Which one goes on which foot?"

"Which shoe do you think goes on which foot?" I asked.

"I don't know," she said. "I just can't tell."

"Did you match the curves?"

"Yes, and it didn't help."

"Keep trying," I coached. "You can do it."

But, Allyson was over it. She picked up her shoes and said, "I'll just carry them."

"Nah, I'll help you," I comforted, putting her right shoe on first, and then her left. "You'll get it eventually, babe."

I sighed a big sigh, realizing we hadn't experienced the

monumental breakthrough that morning that I thought we had.

Later that night, with homework and baths completed, the girls slipped on their pjs and piled onto our bed, awaiting Daddy's bedtime story and prayer time.

"G'night, Mommy," Abby said, before heading down the hallway to her room.

"Night, Sweetie."

"'night, Mommy. Love you," Allyson said, giving me a hug and a kiss.

As I gave her a hug in return, I glanced down at her bunny slippers. Their ears were pointing the wrong way, meaning just one thing, Allyson hadn't yet figured out which one went on which foot.

I didn't say a word; I just smiled and hugged her again.

We're a lot like that as we grow up in the Lord. There are many days when I can't figure out "which shoe goes on which foot"—especially when it comes to being a mom and making the best decisions for my children. I'll look at the situation, and like Allyson, I'll try and match it with the right solution. Sometimes I may study that situation for days, weeks, and even months. Finally, in frustration, I'll abandon the problem like Allyson did, and pick up my shoes and carry them.

I wonder how many times I've gone boldly into the throne room with the ears on my bunny slippers pointing the wrong direction, and how many times God has just smiled and hugged me anyway.

So, if you're struggling with something in your life today, and you just can't figure out "which one goes on which foot," God's got you covered. No problem, no situation, no challenge is too big for our God. He loves you, and He wants to help.

KISSES FROM HEAVEN

If any of you lacks wisdom, you should ask God, who gives generously to all without finding fault, and it will be given to you.

James 1:5 (NIV)

HEART TO HEAVEN

God, thank You for loving me despite my shortcomings. Thank You for being patient with me as I grow up in You, and help me to show that same patience with my children. In the Name of Jesus, Amen.

Chapter 49

NO MORE MICROMANAGING

Abby, my oldest daughter, has always wanted to be a teacher. Even when she was a little girl, she would line up her stuffed animals and pretend to be their teacher. And, she's extremely gifted with children. I often call her the Pied Piper of kiddos because no matter where we are, somehow children find her and interact with her. It's obviously a calling for her, but after one year of studying elementary education in college, Abby started questioning her chosen career path. Instead of letting her express her concerns and lending an understanding ear, I swooped in to micromanage. I began asking her to consider a political science major with a possible double major in marketing. I told her she'd do so well as a "chief of staff" for a senator because of her outgoing personality and superior organizational and problem-solving skills.

By the end of the day, I had pretty much secured an internship for her in a senator's office for that summer. I was on it . . . but I shouldn't have been.

In hindsight, I should have let Abby voice her concerns about her elementary education major, tell her she was equipped and well able to succeed in that career, and then hit my knees to pray for her as she struggled with her calling. Instead, I helped her transfer colleges to one that had a strong Political Science program, moved her several thousand miles into her new college, helped her decorate her dorm room, and headed home so proud of myself for being a supportive mother. I so shouldn't have been proud of myself.

After one semester at this college that was too far from home for Abby's liking, taking classes in a new major that she knew in her heart wasn't her calling, Abby transferred to Indiana University (about thirty minutes from our home) to once again pursue a career in education. It ended up costing her about a year's worth of credits and us about $19,000.

Yep, that lesson was learned the hard way for both of us.

After that incident (and a pint of double fudge ice cream), I realized that I might actually need to join a support group. "Hi, my name is Michelle Medlock Adams, and I am a micromanaging mom."

Be honest . . . do you need to join that same support group?

Dictionary.com defines micromanage as: "to manage or control with excessive attention to minor details." That pretty much sums up my personality—especially when it comes to my daughters. I think I was a helicopter mom before the term existed, but my heart was always in the right place. I tried to "handle" everything for my girls, thinking I could save them from making costly mistakes. I wanted to protect their hearts from being hurt. I wanted to shelter them from all of life's storms, but you know what I learned? That's not possible. Not only is it not possible, but also it's not good. Because sometimes, we have to learn things the hard way—by going through it. Plus, I also discovered that I'm not always right.

Imagine that.

So, if you, too, are a bit of a micromanager, take it from me: it's best to let God be the only micromanager in the household. You'll discover that He is way better at it than you are, and your children will be much happier if you back off a bit—or in my case, a lot. And, you'll be much happier, too. Micromanaging is a frustrating, all-consuming, thankless job, and one that you were never intended to do so leave it to the Master Micromanager and go back to being just "Mom."

KISSES FROM HEAVEN

*Cast all your anxiety on him because
he cares for you.*

1 Peter 5:7 (NIV)

HEART TO HEAVEN

Father, help me to fully trust You with my children,
and help me to be more of a prayer warrior than
a micromanager. I love You and praise You. In the
mighty name of Jesus, Amen.

Chapter 50

THE MOST EXHAUSTING, REWARDING JOB EVER

As mothers, whether we realize it or not, we live for our children. In the beginning, it's all about meeting their basic needs: feeding them, bathing them, rocking them to sleep, changing their poopy diapers, and praying you can squeeze in a shower before nightfall. As our kiddos grow, we become their chauffeurs, their Scout leaders, their homework helpers, their room moms, their coaches, their chocolate chip cookie bakers, and so much more. When they reach high school, our roles change a bit as our children gain more independence, but we're still the ones sitting in the bleachers or the auditorium cheering them on, or chaperoning their school dances (much to their embarrassment), or helping them fill out college applications, or hosting pizza parties for all of their friends.

It's what we do and it's who we are.

It's the most exhausting, aggravating, fulfilling job you'll ever have, and it all goes by in a big blur of wonderfulness. And when the hustle and bustle of graduation is over and you're helping them move into their college dorm rooms, reality sets in.

Your nest is empty forever.

I had that reality meltdown moment as we boarded the shuttle bound for LAX and left my youngest daughter, Ally, waving to us from the curb outside her student housing in Los Angeles. I could see she was holding back tears, but I wasn't as brave. I blubbered the entire shuttle ride and most of the four-and-a-half-hour flight back to Indiana. It wasn't that I was sad to be left alone with my husband, Jeff. I still really liked him, even after 22 years of marriage, I just didn't know who I was or what purpose I would serve without my girls.

Grabbing my hand on the flight, he whispered, "It's going to be OK. You've done a great job with our girls. They're ready."

The problem was, I wasn't ready! I wanted more time. I wanted more prom-dress shopping trips. I wanted more late-night movie marathons. I wanted more cheerleading competitions. I wanted more Powder Puff football. I wanted . . . more.

My favorite job—the one I'd loved for more than 20 years—was over. At least that's what I thought when I returned to our house, empty except for the three cats and two dachshunds that greeted me as I put down my bag.

Just then, my cell phone vibrated. It was a text from Ally: "I miss you and Dad already. I know you're sad, but don't be, Mom. We'll still see each other on breaks. I love you so much. You'll always be my best friend."

I wiped away the tears just in time to read another text coming through, from my college sophomore, Abby, who had just transferred to a Christian college in Florida: "Hey Mom, can we Skype tonight? I need some face time with you."

It was as if God was letting me know my Mom job wasn't over. My girls still needed me, and they always would. As I finished texting back both daughters, Jeff rounded the corner.

"Wanna go to bed early and watch movies?" he asked, smiling at me with the same smile I'd fallen in love with back in high school.

"Sure," I answered.

As I grabbed my bag and headed upstairs, it seemed my nest was empty, but my heart was full. And, I'm happy to report, it's still full and my girls still need me, and Jeff and I are enjoying this empty-nesting situation much more than we thought we would. We're sort of like honeymooners again!

No matter what phase of mommyhood you're currently enjoying, treasure every moment. Drink it in. Take lots of pictures. Make lots of memories. Pray lots of prayers. And, just know that the nest is never truly empty. My beautiful birdies find their way home quite often, and your birdies will, too.

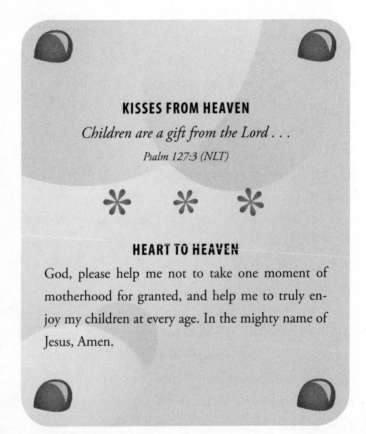

KISSES FROM HEAVEN

Children are a gift from the Lord . . .
Psalm 127:3 (NLT)

✳   ✳   ✳

HEART TO HEAVEN

God, please help me not to take one moment of motherhood for granted, and help me to truly enjoy my children at every age. In the mighty name of Jesus, Amen.

Michelle Medlock Adams is an award-winning journalist and best-selling author, earning top honors from the Associated Press, the Society of Professional Journalists, and the Hoosier State Press Association. She is an author of over 60 books and more than 1,000 articles for newspapers and magazines since graduating with a journalism degree from Indiana University. Her book *God Knows You* won "The SELAH Award" for best children's book in 2014 and "Book of the Year" for 2014.

Michelle ghostwrites books for celebrities and some of today's most effective and popular ministers. She is also a much sought after teacher at writers conferences and universities around the nation.

Michelle is married to her high school sweetheart, Jeff, and they have two college-aged daughters, Abby and Allyson, as well as a small petting zoo. When not writing or teaching writing, Michelle enjoys teaching fitness classes at her local gym and cheering on Indiana University sports teams, the Chicago Cubbies, and the LA Kings.